A PRIMARY T
GUIDE

RE
and
Collective
Worship

Geoff Teece

Nash Pollock
Publishing

Dedication

To my Mother and Father

© Geoff Teece

First published 2001

Published by
Nash Pollock Publishing
32 Warwick Street
Oxford OX4 1SX

10 9 8 7 6 5 4 3 2 1

Orders to:
York Publishing Services
64 Hallfield Road
Layerthorpe
York YO31 7ZQ

A catalogue record of this book is available from the British Library.

ISBN: 1 898255 36 9

Design and typesetting by Black Dog Design, Buckingham
Printed in Great Britain by T J International Ltd, Padstow

Contents

Introduction 1

1 What is RE? 2
Religious education and the National Curriculum 2
What are the aims of RE? 2
Formulating an aim for RE 6

2 What is religion? 13
The difficulty of finding a definition 14
Religion and religions 21

3 Process and planning in RE 24
Thinking about the process of RE 24
Thinking about planning RE topics 28
Approaches to planning RE 34

4 Assessment 43
The purpose and principles of assessment 43
Planning and assessment 45
Standards in RE 58
Recording achievement in RE 62
Conclusion 63

5 The teacher's role 65
Commitment and the RE teacher 65
Dealing with controversial issues, including pupil's questions 67
Professional knowledge and abilities 68
The RE co-ordinator 73

6   Using stories   75
    Why tell stories in RE?   75
    What kinds of stories are suitable for RE?   77
    Choosing the 'right' stories   78
    Preparing a story   84
    Telling a story   85
    Two examples: The Easter Story for Key Stage 1   86
    *   Using a modern fable at Key Stage 2* 90

7   Visiting places of worship   96
    Advice on visiting places of worship   97

8   Using visual resources   102
    Artefacts   102
    Using pictures for teaching   106
    Useful sources for artefacts and pictures   109
    RE and the internet   111
    Videos   113

9   Collective worship   114
    The relationship between RE and collective worship   114
    Collective worship: statutory requirements   116
    Collective worship: towards an inclusive understanding 117
    Collective worship: practical issues   121
    Inspection and collective worship   124

    Glossary   125

    Bibliography   130

List of figures

1 The purpose of RE?   3
2 Example aims from post 1988 agreed syllabuses   11
3 Teachers' responses to 'What is religion?'   13
4 The content of 'Field of Enquiry' of RE   26
5 The process of RE   27
6 Identifying appropriate questions in the context of the
   Muslim tradition   30
7 Concepts within the six major traditions   31
8 Concepts derived from human experience   32
9 Concepts derived from the study of religion   33
10 Outline of a systems approach   34
11 Outline of a human experience approach   39
12 Categories of human experience   41
13 What is assessment for?   44
14 Attitudes in RE   46
15 Skills in RE   47
16 Units of work for Year 6 – 'Why are we here?'   50
17 Birmingham Agreed Syllabus –
   End of Key Stage descriptions   52
18 Units of work for Year 2 – 'Loving and Giving'   54
19 Steps approach – Staffordshire Agreed Syllabus   56
20 The language of learning objectives   58
21 An example of formative assessment for Year 6 unit of work   59
22 Evaluations of inter-faith study courses   67
23 Lesson plan: 'Why are we here?'   70
24 Types of effective questions   71
25 A checklist of questions   72
26 An example of using a Bible story in Key Stages 1 and 2   80
27 Reasons for visiting places of worship   96
28 Exploring the process of RE through pictures   109
29 Statutory requirements for collective worship   116
30 Debating points for collective worship   118
31 Educational opportunities provided by collective worship   120
32 Ways of organising collective worship   121

Acknowledgements

I would like to thank the following for their help with this book: my colleagues Jill Maybury for the list of stories in Chapter 6, and Camilla O'Connor for preparing the difficult bits of the manuscript! Three of my PGCE trainees, Tracey Cole, Cherith Reid and Ben Dunlop for the list of websites contained in Chapter 8. Paul Bellingham, RE Adviser for Staffordshire, for permission to use the 'steps' approach in Chapter 4. The table 'Categories of human experience' is developed from an original published in *How do I Teach RE?* by Garth Read *et al* and the lesson plan proforma in Chapter 5 is based on an original by Michael Grimmitt. Finally, thanks go to my former colleagues at Westhill - Garth Read, John Rudge and Roger Howarth for their friendship, vision and expertise.

Introduction

This book is written for primary school RE co-ordinators, those who wish to become co-ordinators, and primary teachers in training. There are quite a lot of books available for the primary RE co-ordinator. Such books are often very helpful in a practical way. They introduce the co-ordinator to legislation about RE and its place in the primary curriculum, and provide helpful guidance on such important aspects of planning and assessing RE as well as appropriate approaches to teaching and resourcing the subject. At the present time attention has been given to the requirements of being a subject leader in RE. A helpful publication about this role is a booklet produced by the Association of RE Inspectors, Advisers and Consultants (AREIAC), *Effective Subject Leadership in Religious Education*.[1] That publication deals extensively with the requirements of being a manager of the subject. It provides a helpful means of monitoring the co-ordinator's role as a subject leader.

However, while this book addresses some of the practical aspects of the job, it is also designed to do something else. One of the characteristics of some of the books for RE co-ordinators is that they tend to take subject knowledge as a given. However, most primary teachers know that this is an area where they need most help. This is also true of primary RE trainees who in their PGCE courses receive only a minimum of subject knowledge during their course. Therefore an attempt has been made in this book to address some of the concerns for help with subject knowledge. Subject knowledge in RE is a complex area. Some see it as becoming more familiar with the teachings and practices of the major religious traditions. While this is important, and there is some information about the traditions contained in this book, a teacher with good subject knowledge not only knows something about the religions but understands something about the nature of religion itself and how such knowledge can be applied to the process of teaching and learning in the subject. Arguably a degree of mastery of this will help practitioners become a better planner and teacher of the subject. Therefore an attempt has been made to help the reader think more deeply and clearly about this important aspect of teaching RE.

---

[1] Grove, Julie and Teece Geoff, *Effective Subject Leadership in Religious Education*, Association of RE Advisors, Inspectors and Consultants, 1999

1 What is RE?

Religious education and the National Curriculum

The 1988 Education Reform Act requires that RE, like the National Curriculum core subjects, must be provided in all schools for all pupils in every year in which they attend school. However, RE holds a unique position in the curriculum: it is the only compulsory subject that is not governed by National Curriculum orders and assessment arrangements. Instead, the legal requirements for the RE curriculum and assessment arrangements in local authority schools are decided at regional level. These requirements are published as the local agreed syllabus for RE.

This basis is derived from the 1944 Education Act and was reaffirmed in the 1988 Education Reform Act. The 1988 Act recognised the developments which had taken place in the subject since 1944 inasmuch as it stated that any agreed syllabus published after 1988 should reflect the multi-faith nature of society, while giving due regard to the position and influence of the Christian tradition.

What are the aims of RE?

There are varying views as to what the aims of RE should be. This is partly due to the fact that RE for many people is bound up with personal values which are dearly held, in that their religion is the most important thing in their lives. The idea of religious education, therefore, can raise strong emotions and fixed positions. Uncertainty about RE may also stem from the two words which comprise its title: religion and education. Both of these words represent what can be called contested concepts. This means that it is possible to disagree about what we mean by the terms. For example, is education about developing whole persons, a form of human development, or is it merely a utilitarian enterprise designed to fit people for the world of work? Religion is just as complex. Does it make sense to talk about something called religion which exists independently of individual religions, as some kind of universal phenomenon into which we should initiate children, or can we only talk about the Christian religion, the Hindu religion and so on – in which case the question centres around how many of these religions we should teach children about. Alternatively we could take the view that this latter possibility is not religious education at all, and that if religious education is to be religious then children should be taught to *be* Christians, Hindus etc. Of course this view highlights a key dilemma within RE. On which of the two words should the emphasis lie, religion or education?

These may seem like big and intractable questions to the busy primary teacher, but it is essential to have opportunities to discuss such questions. Here is a discussion exercise which attempts to get at the heart of these issues about the nature of RE:

Consider the statements below, and try and identify how far and in what way you agree or disagree with such views. You might like to note what is acceptable to you and why. Additionally, you might like to consider how these statements stand as complete views of RE.

The purpose of RE is   to make children Christian

                               to make children moral

                               to reinforce children in their own faith

Or

The purpose of RE is   to teach children about the religions of the world

                               to help children become more tolerant in our religiously plural society

                               to help children develop their own ideas and values

---

Figure 1: The purpose of RE?

Quite clearly, any comment on these statements must begin with reference to the Education Reform Act of 1988. With regard to RE, the Act says that any agreed syllabus published after 1988 must

- reflect the fact that the religious traditions in Great Britain are in the main Christian, and
- take account of the teachings and practices of the other principal religious traditions represented in Great Britain.[1]

It is fascinating to explore how this situation came about. This can be done by taking an historical perspective on the development of the agreed syllabus since the 1944 Act. Before we do that, however, it is worth commenting on the statements above.

Is the purpose of RE to make children Christian?

Obviously there are people who hold this view. In a similar way there are people who hold the view that the purpose of RE is to make children Muslim, Jewish, Sikh, etc. The first thing to say about such a view is that it is not provided for in the 1988 Act. In addition, many teachers react strongly to forcing anyone into a religious belief of any kind. There are several reasons for this. First, in a plural and increasingly secular society such a view would be offensive to some parents and teachers. In a secular context, teaching children to accept the Christian faith would be regarded by many as indoctrination. It might be a legitimate aim of a voluntary aided church school, but is at odds with the plural nature of many state-maintained schools, particularly in our bigger towns and cities. Moreover, any attempt to force a religion on a group of pupils would quite naturally cause offence to the considerable number of pupils from a variety of other religious backgrounds. Secondly, it is difficult to see how one can teach anybody to accept any beliefs and values without willingness on behalf of the learner. If this willingness is absent, we may be guilty of indoctrination.

Is the purpose of RE to make children 'moral'?

Most teachers reply to this statement, 'Whose morals?' It seems there is a difficulty with this view, not only because of the complex question of whether there really is agreement in society about shared values, but also because many would question whether it is possible to teach children to be 'moral' or good.

Secondly, whilst we must recognise that all religions have a moral dimension, learning only about that aspect is not enough.

Thirdly, if the teaching of morals is a task that the school should engage in, and it is difficult to see how this aspect is not to be addressed in some way, this is a task for the whole of schooling. There are moral dimensions to all subjects, as well as the part that moral values play in the general ethos of the school and the hidden curriculum. To ally morality too closely to religious education as a school subject is both limiting and misguided.

Is the purpose of RE to reinforce children in their own faith?

Unlike the first approach which we considered, there is no possibility here of imposing what is inappropriate on our pupils. In fact, the statement implies that we recognise fully the pluralistic nature of society. However, while we may wish to assert that RE must take into account the variety of pupils' religious backgrounds, it is the role of the family and the religious community to 'bring children up' in the faith. It is not the job of the maintained school, though, as we mentioned above, it may well be the job of the voluntary school along with the family and religious community to nurture children in their faith. That is why, for example, it is seen as appropriate for children attending a Roman Catholic primary school to hear mass on a regular basis. This is not allowed in law for maintained schools. It also explains why RE and collective worship are governed by different regulations in voluntary aided schools, and to some extent in voluntary controlled schools.

Is the purpose of RE to teach children about the religions of the world?

Many teachers might wish to support this view, but it is not without its difficulties.

Firstly, detractors point to the possibility of confusion (often referred to as a mish-mash) in pupils' minds if they are presented with too much information about too many religions. There is no easy answer to this issue but we deal with it in appropriate detail in Chapters 2 and 3.

Secondly, it is generally agreed that RE is about more than merely providing information about religions. For example, questions need to be raised such as:

• How do pupils interact with the knowledge they gain?
• What is the relevance of the study of religions to the personal development of pupils?

It would seem that just teaching children about religions, though necessary, is not sufficient on its own.

However, it is important to stress this learning about religions as an important aspect of RE, not least because historically, primary RE has tended to neglect it. However, the same questions remain as to what exactly we are teaching when we talk about teaching children about religion or religions. We deal with this in some detail in Chapter 2.

Is the purpose of RE to help children become more tolerant?

This statement is primarily concerned with attitudes rather than knowledge. But any attitude must be built on knowledge, so perhaps this view answers some of the queries raised by the previous views. However, 'tolerant' is a difficult word; it has overtones of 'tolerate' (that is, of 'putting up with them now that they are here'). Indeed some commentators on the wording of the 1988 Act where it refers to 'taking account of' the teachings and practices of the other (non-Christian) religious traditions, have made a similar criticism. This view holds that the authors of the Act were concerned with transmitting Christian values, which, the authors would claim, underpin the values of our society. However, in a kind of reluctant acceptance of the plural nature of society, they then urge schools to 'take account of' the other traditions – though it is assumed (so the argument goes) that values will be transmitted through the Christian tradition.

A generous reading of this statement, however, would interpret 'tolerant' to include understanding and openness towards others. This, we would want to say, is a laudable aim but insufficient on its own. It clearly requires refining with appropriate knowledge.

Is the purpose of RE to help children develop their own ideas and values?

The 1988 Act says that all pupils should receive an education that promotes their spiritual and moral development (amongst other things) and prepares them for adult life. So this view, like the previous one, may go some way towards answering the questions we posed about the relevance of the study of religions to the personal development of pupils. We would want to support this view, in the sense that children need to learn to 'think for themselves', while recognising that it requires some explaining.

A criticism of this particular view, as it stands, might be that it smacks somewhat of individualism, the danger of which is that it may relativise all values. In the most extreme cases this view might come to represent the point of view characterised by 'what's right for me is right'.

While recognising the importance of personal autonomy, we would not want to equate that with a notion of freedom that ignores personal responsibility.

Whatever the importance of personal autonomy, it is quite clear that helping children to develop their own beliefs and values is not the sole preserve of RE.

Formulating an aim for RE

Historical perspectives: The development of the agreed syllabus

We can learn a lot about how the subject has developed and changed, and hence what it is today, by examining the development of the agreed syllabus.

This locally determined basis for RE is derived from the 1944 Education Act and has been reaffirmed in the 1988 Act. However, the 1944 Act assumed several things, including the belief that RE was about the teaching of Christianity either in a denominational form, in the case of Voluntary Aided schools, or in broadly Christian terms. This notion of 'broadly Christian' has its origins in a dispute that took place in the early part of the nineteenth century. Before the Education Act of 1870 the Church had almost complete control of education in this country. However, with the advent of the Industrial Revolution the towns were becoming heavily populated and the state began to provide education through its Board Schools. This in turn lead to a controversy about the place of Christian teaching in these new schools. Dr Andrew Bell, an Anglican, favoured the kind of teaching which took place in the church schools, which was essentially Church teaching according to the catechism. Joseph Lancaster, a Quaker, differed from Dr Bell in favouring the non-sectarian teaching of what he called 'general Christian principles and them only'. It is in this disagreement that we can trace the roots of the different requirements for voluntary church and state maintained schools that we have in law today.

The dispute was, in a sense, formalised with the passing of the 1870 Education Act. This act sought to provide both for education which took place in provided schools funded by the state through the Board of Education, and for non-provided schools which were the preserve of Church organisations, largely the Church of England, the Roman Catholic Church, and some nonconformist churches. While denominational teaching could take place in the non-provided schools, teaching in the provided schools was governed by the Cowper Temple Clause. This stated that 'no religious catechism or formulary distinctive of any particular denomination shall be taught.' Therefore from 1870 onwards we had a dual system of education with regard to the place of teaching religion in schools.

The 1944 Act made religious teaching compulsory. It also echoed the controversy of 1870 about broadly Christian teaching. Because there wasn't, necessarily, a consensus about what this 'broadly Christian teaching' could mean, and because there were greater divisions than today between the different Christian denominations, it was decided that a national consensus on RE was unworkable.

Local agreed syllabuses for RE existed before 1944 but the 1944 Act made it compulsory for every local authority to have one. In other words the Act stated that RE must be provided for locally by means of a syllabus which was to be agreed by an Agreed Syllabus Conference. This body was to consist of four groups, representing the Church of England, other Christian denominations, teachers and the local authority.

Early agreed syllabuses
CambridgeshireLocal Education Authority produced an agreed syllabus as early as 1924. At the time it was very influential. It was also very much a product of its time both in content and purpose. In terms of content it was biblical, and the purpose of teaching was described in the syllabus as 'not simply to present the Bible as a record of historical events but to bring children into an encounter with Jesus Christ'.[2] The introduction to the *Handbook* which was written to accompany the syllabus says, 'The Gospels were the manuals of preacher and teacher in carrying their message from one land to another and from one generation to the next. Our business in religious teaching is the same.'[3] The *Handbook* recognises the force of the Cowper Temple Clause of 1870 in terms of denominational teaching and seeks to avoid denominational controversy, but the assumption is confessional; albeit a broadly based one. Being a biblically based syllabus it is fair to say that its focus was on the past. Early syllabuses were, largely, syllabuses for scripture lessons. The intention of such lessons was the nurturing of pupils' spiritual lives within the context of a common Christian heritage. Such intentions were clearly expressed in the Surrey syllabus of 1945:

> 'The aim of the Syllabus is to secure that children attending the schools of the County ... may gain knowledge of the common Christian faith held by their fathers for nearly 2,000 years; may seek for themselves in Christianity principles which give a purpose to life and a guide to all its problems; and may find inspiration, power and courage to work for their own welfare, for that of their fellow creatures, and for the growth of God's kingdom.'[4]

Agreed syllabuses in the 1960s
The single most significant influence on syllabuses of the 1960s was the influence on education in general of cognitive stage development theory, particularly the work of Jean Piaget. As far as RE was concerned, Piaget's work formed the theoretical foundation of the research of Ronald Goldman, who wrote two significant books, *Religious Thinking from Childhood to Adolescence* and *Readiness for Religion*.[5] The second title was characteristic of the period, which saw the word 'readiness' figure in the titles in other subject areas, for example *Readiness for Reading*. The concept of 'readiness', derived from the findings of Piaget, was famously described by the American educationalist Jerome Bruner as a 'half truth'.

The half that is true is the view that curriculum planning and teaching approaches must take into consideration the developmental needs of the pupils. The half which is not true is the view that a teacher cannot do anything to accelerate a pupil's 'readiness'. This general educational debate found its way into the consciousness of Agreed Syllabus conferences in the 1960s. The most influential of the time was the syllabus produced by the West Riding of Yorkshire. Published in 1966, this syllabus took seriously the work of people like Goldman. A section on the underlying principles of the syllabus states, 'The material in the syllabus must be related to life and experience. An attempt has been made to introduce reality and relevance into all sections of the syllabus.'⁶ Consequently the syllabus develops a thematic approach, especially in the early years of schooling. In truth the approach can be more accurately described as experiential religious education. This approach, which was developed at Westhill College, Birmingham by Ronald Goldman and Douglas Huberry, sought to relate the ordinary experience of children to the Bible. This approach also became known as the 'life theme approach', although strictly speaking the life theme approach differed from experiential RE in that it emphasised that human experience as well as the Biblical material was worth studying in its own right. Apart from the 'relevance' aspect, this syllabus was significant for the fact that it included two pages with reference to non-Christian religions. This would be described as 'tokenism' today but it is an early indication of a growing awareness of the existence of children in schools from non-Christian backgrounds.

Implicit and explicit RE
These two dimensions to the West Riding syllabus lead the way to significant developments in RE during the later 1960s and early 1970s. Goldman's work was becoming highly influential and it left a legacy of both positive and negative influences. The positive, as we have seen, was the emphasis on needing to consider carefully the ways in which children actually learn. The negative influences, at the time, included the watering down of explicit religious material for the primary years because it was assumed that young children found religious material too difficult.

Partly due to this, and partly due to influences from Christian theology as well as an increasing presence in society of people from other countries, there grew up in the 1970s a distinction between what has been called 'implicit RE' and 'explicit RE'. Implicit RE, which became popular in primary schools, concerned itself with children's own experiences, feelings, emotions and insights, especially in terms of relationships. By concentrating on these things it was hoped that children would become sensitive towards and ask questions about 'human experience understood at depth'. This notion was discussed at length by a number of continental theologians, especially Paul Tillich[7], but is perhaps most clearly expressed by M V C Jeffreys when he said: 'Religious truth is normal experience understood at depth'.[8] The implicit approach would encourage children to consider general concepts such as love, care and honesty, usually through thematic work such as 'homes' and 'families'. Unlike the experiential approach, the introduction of religious or biblical material was not deemed to be necessary. To explore these human experience concepts at depth was enough for such an approach to count as religious.

The explicit approach concentrated on religion as an observable phenomenon in the world. It was much influenced by the work of Professor Ninian Smart who saw religion in terms of six, and eventually seven, dimensions. In other words if we were to study any religious tradition we could study it in terms of its ritual, its narrative and mythology, its doctrine and philosophy, its ethics, its social institutions, its works of art, religious buildings etc, and the personal experience of its adherents[9]. In terms of its application to RE this underpinning led to a concentration on aspects such as festivals, rites of passage, pilgrimage, sacred books, founders of religions and so on.

These two dimensions ran side by side in the 1970s but were rarely integrated. In the early years of schooling in particular, the implicit approach was seen as a foundation for the later understanding of the more explicit aspects of religion. In practice there developed an approach to primary RE that concentrated almost solely on the implicit to the exclusion of the explicit. Themes such as 'caring' and practices such as having pets in the classroom, whilst dealing with important aspects of human experience, did so with little or no reference to religions. In the most extreme cases it was possible to imagine that the removal of RE from the curriculum would make little or no difference to what went on. A subject called social studies or personal, social and moral education could quite easily embrace such an approach. Likewise any concentration on the explicit tended to do so in a way that divorced the study of religion from the concerns of human experience. There was a danger of explicit RE becoming a collection of strange customs and observances that bore little relevance and relationship to children's own existential concerns.

The Birmingham Agreed Syllabus, 1975
The Birmingham syllabus was the next 'landmark' syllabus. It was so on two counts: it was the first syllabus to describe its content in terms of the

six major world religions, and hence became the first truly multi-faith syllabus; and in its introduction, if not in its programme of study, it sought to describe how the implicit and explicit dimensions could be integrated. On page 4 it states, 'The syllabus should be used to enlarge and deepen children's understanding of religion by studying world religions and by exploring all those elements of human experience which raise questions about life's ultimate meaning and value'[10].

The 1980s onwards: a growing consensus
During the 1980s and into the 1990s a general consensus has developed among compilers of agreed syllabuses as to what we should be aiming for in RE. Let us look at some examples here.

The Agreed Syllabus for RE, Waltham Forest 1988

The principal aim of Religious Education is to enable pupils to understand, reflect upon and respond to the religious and spiritual beliefs, practices, insights and experiences that are expressed in humanity's search for meaning in life. Also, to provide opportunities for pupils to explore their own beliefs.

The Agreed Syllabus for RE, Oxfordshire 1993

Aims of Religious Education

1 To be aware of and respond to life experiences and the questions they raise

2 To know about and understand religious beliefs and practices

3 To evaluate the significance of religious concepts, beliefs and practices by being able to express personal opinions based on the use of appropriate evidence and argument

---

The Agreed Syllabus for RE, Redbridge 1995

The aim of Religious Education is to promote the spiritual, moral, social, cultural and intellectual development of pupils by encouraging them to explore and respond to those aspects of religion and human experience, which raise fundamental questions of belief and value.

Figure 2: Example aims from post-1988 agreed syllabuses

In 1994 the Schools Curriculum and Assessment Authority (now QCA) published what have come to be known as Model Syllabuses for RE. This resulted from a concern by government that those who are responsible for producing agreed syllabuses should receive as much guidance as possible, especially about what to teach at each key stage. Groups representing the six major religions met to decide what about their faith they would wish pupils to learn. Their deliberations were published as two 'models', *Living Faiths* and *Questions and Teachings*[11]. All sorts of issues about RE arose from this exercise but this is not the place to go into them. It is, however, important to point out that these 'model syllabuses' have no jurisdiction in school. The legal document which must inform school planning is the local agreed syllabus or, in the case of a voluntary school, the Diocesan syllabus.

Recent agreed syllabuses reflect a growing consensus about RE which places emphasis on three distinct but interrelated areas. Firstly, and obviously, RE is about enabling pupils to develop a knowledge and understanding of religion. Secondly, RE should enable pupils to explore fundamental questions arising out of our human experience of life. Thirdly, RE should enable pupils to develop their own visions of life arising partly out of their studies.

These three areas, which can be referred to as the 'field of enquiry' for RE should form the basis of good curriculum planning in RE. What this actually means and how it can be conceptualised in terms of planning and teaching is the subject of the next two chapters.

[1] Education Reform Act 1988, Chapter 40 section 8, HMSO
[2] Cambridge, *The Cambridge Syllabus of Religious Teaching for Schools*, Cambridgeshire and Isle of Ely Education Committee, 1939
[3] Yeaxlee, Basil, *Handbook to the Cambridgeshire Syllabus of Religious Teaching for Schools*, SCM, 1940, page 10
[4] Surrey, *Syllabus for Religious Instruction*, Surrey County Council Education Committee, 1945
[5] Goldman, Ronald, *Religious Thinking from Childhood to Adolescence*, Routledge, 1964, and *Readiness for Religion*, Routledge 1965
[6] West Riding, *Suggestions for Religious Education: The West Riding Agreed Syllabus*, County Council of the West Riding of Yorkshire Education Department, 1966
[7] Tillich, Paul, *The Shaking of the Foundations*, Penguin, 1962
[8] Jeffreys M V C, *Glaucon: An Inquiry into the Aims of Education*, Pitman, 1955
[9] Smart, Ninian, *The Phenomenon of Religion*, Macmillan, 1973
[10] Birmingham, *Agreed Syllabus of Religious Instruction*, City of Birmingham Education Committee, 1975
[11] QCA, *Model Syllabuses for RE*, Model 1 *Living Faiths Today*, Model 2 *Questions and Teaching*, School Curriculum and Assessment Authority, 1994

2 What is religion?

What is it that we should be teaching in RE? This has been a perennial question for RE teachers to attempt to answer. A music teacher teaches music, a science teacher teaches science and so on. If we say an RE teacher teaches religion, what does that mean? Does it mean we teach children about religion? If so, what do we mean by religion? Do we mean a particular religion? Or do we mean a variety of religions, or do we mean that we teach about something called religion, of which the religions are particular forms? Obviously we can't begin to answer that question until we know what we mean by the term religion. What we can say is that successful teachers possess a good knowledge of their subject. Unfortunately very few primary teachers are given the opportunity to explore questions to do with the nature of religion in their training. Therefore, before we consider in detail what to teach and how to plan it, we need to consider this question of what, in general, the term religion might mean.

It might be worth pausing for a minute to ask what you understand by the term religion. It is not an easy question. Does any definition of religion require a mention of God? But where does that leave Buddhists, whose religion is not based on belief in God?

On a recent in-service course I asked a group of primary RE co-ordinators to write down what the term 'religion' meant to them. There were a wide variety of responses, including the following:

Religion is

Believing in God

Looking after one's soul

Love for others

Tradition

Obligation

Culture and community

Customs and rules

Worship, rituals and celebrations

Personal faith

Something which gives meaning to life

A way of life

Something which answers questions for people

Figure 3: Teachers' responses to 'What is Religion?'

The difficulty of finding a definition

As the list shows, there are many ways in which we can try and define religion. Traditionally there have been many ways in which religion has been studied. Religion has been studied by psychologists, sociologists, historians, anthropologists and, of course, theologians. However, one of the problems we have is that none of these approaches, on its own, appears to provide a satisfactory basis for RE. If we think about religion from a sociological perspective, for example, our teaching may become sociological in character. Therefore we teach children about human groups, community and so on but our teaching may fail to bring out the spiritual significance of religion. If we try and understand religion from a historical perspective then we run the risk of teaching children history and not RE. For example, is a topic on how Christianity came to Britain an RE topic or a history topic? What characteristics will make it one sort of topic rather than another?

The problem doesn't get any easier when we come to theology. We might assume that understanding religion theologically is the right approach. Maybe the teacher who said religion is 'Believing in God' is taking a theological approach. However, believing in God is something which characterises some religions and some religious people. It doesn't for example characterise some Buddhists and, of course, it depends on what we mean by God. If we mean belief in a personal God with whom one can form a relationship, in a sense that many Christians would understand, then 'Believing in God' doesn't apply to some Hindus. The problem with a theological approach is that theology has traditionally been confessional and confined to a particular tradition, for example Christian theology or Islamic theology. In other words Christians have tended to study Christian theology, Muslims Islamic theology and so on, with little or no concern for other traditions. In some ways this mirrors the situation with which we are faced in RE. For many years RE teaching was a convergent activity. This means that it was seen as a Christian confessional enterprise, which assumed Christian teachers were teaching Christianity to tomorrow's Christian adults. We are clearly not in a position, either practically or morally, to do that in today's state schools if we wish to provide an inclusive religious education for all our pupils.

In the academic world there have been some interesting moves to fashion a kind of world theology which eventually might provide a firm theoretical base on which to build a modern RE programme. In the meantime we have to ask ourselves the question, 'Is there a way of understanding and studying religion which is neither naturalistic (derived from one of the disciplines mentioned such as sociology) and, therefore by implication unconcerned with the spirituality of religion, nor confessional, which we have agreed is not appropriate?

If we look again at the statements offered by the in-service group above, one way of responding to the statements would be to see whether it is possible to put them into categories or groups. One distinction that we could make is between statements like 'Something that gives meaning to life' and 'Worship, rituals and celebrations'. The former could be said to be an attempt at explaining why religion is important for people. Perhaps it also hints at the spiritual significance of religion: that it gives life meaning. The second statement refers, in a general sense, to practices which we associate with the phenomena of religion. These practices become particular when we study individual religions because each religion has its own particular forms of worship, ritual and celebration. It could be said that it is the worship, rituals and celebrations that provide the means by which religious believers can find, as well as express, meaning.

This is a helpful start to our quest to understand religion on its own terms rather than in terms fashioned by other academic disciplines. For example, Karl Marx referred to religion as the 'opium of the people'.[1] Such statements don't get us very far. Marx's comment is, essentially, a sociological view of how, according to the author, religion has its effect in society. It tells us little about what religion is. Fortunately, there have been more useful attempts to define religion for our purposes.

Religion as the Sacred

Rudolph Otto defined religion as 'a unique original feeling of response ... to the numinous'.[2] If 'numinous' is an unfamiliar word, you might find the word 'sacred' more helpful. What was important for Otto was not studying ideas about God and religion but trying to understand types of religious experience.

Another scholar, Mircea Eliade, explored the difference between a sacred and profane experience of the world.[3] Eliade maintained that, historically speaking, humankind has always been religious and has both a profane (or everyday) and sacred experience of the world. He believed that nature, in fact the whole of the cosmos, is a succession of hierophanies, or manifestations of the sacred. In fact the complete secularisation of nature is a fact only for a limited number of modern cultures.

Eliade believed that the study of religion could help people understand the 'mental universe' of what he calls *homo religiosus* (religious man). He didn't believe that the study of the religions in terms of what their beliefs and practices are could on their own achieve this understanding. This is because the religions have been tainted, so to speak, by years of scholarship. In other words, humanity may get in the way of the divine. He also goes on to say that for many urban dwellers the sense of the sacred has almost totally been lost; and that includes members of religious traditions!

In contrast to modern human beings, whose lives are lived primarily on the mundane or profane level, the ancient person's whole experience of life was capable of being lived in communion with a sacred dimension to existence. According to Eliade this is because the human being of primitive societies did not see his or her nature as 'finished' at birth. In order to become a human in the fullest sense a person must die in his or her natural life and be reborn to a higher life. This higher life is to be found in the ideal image revealed in the mythologies of religions.

According to Eliade, the person who is religious assumes a particular and characteristic mode of existence in the world; and despite the great number of historic religious forms, this characteristic mode is always recognisable. The religious person accepts that life has a sacred origin. This belief is expressed in creation stories. Also the sacred has an absolute reality which transcends the world but is capable of being experienced in the world. This accounts, according to Eliade, for human beings' ability to experience the sacred by way of religious experience. It therefore follows that human existence only realises its potential in so far as it participates in this reality. Finally, according to Eliade, the history of the sacred is preserved in myths.

Profane man, in contrast, refuses transcendence and believes that all life is relative and may even come to doubt that life has any ultimate meaning. Although the great cultures of the past have not been without non-religious humans it is only in the modern West that 'non-religious man' has developed fully. Such development is characterised by Eliade as a 'demysticising' of life. According to this view modern people find the idea of God and its consequent moral and sacred demands as a limit to human freedom. They define themselves not in terms of transcendence but in terms of 'modern' disciplines such as history and science. The historian of religion Wilfred Cantwell Smith[4] echoes Eliade's diagnosis by commenting that the present age is unique in so far as humans define themselves without reference to the transcendent. The German theologian Dietrich Bonhoeffer described this development as 'the world come of age'.[5] This is the modern world where humankind can no longer accept primitive views of God and a universe defined by the sacred. It is the laws of science which hold sway, and religion needs to accommodate itself to this new world if it is to be believable to the modern mind. This view was popularised in this country in the 1960s with the publication of John Robinson's famous book *Honest to God*.[6] Such views, which arose in the earlier part of the twentieth century, became commonly accepted in liberal Christian theological literature in the west. However, as we stand at the dawn of a new century we may be forced to conclude that they are too dismissive of the power of the human quest for the sacred and for something over and above the mundane. Despite frequent reports of falling attendances in the established churches, there are growing evangelical churches; there is a continuing interest in meditation and western forms of Buddhism, as well as Celtic spirituality and new-age philosophies.

It is commonly recognised in the world of religious studies that the history of religion can be viewed in terms of three stages of development. First there is the pre-axial stage sometimes referred to as the *primal stage*. It was, essentially, pre-literate but was characterised by many of the 'sacred' aspects referred to by Eliade. Next came the *axial stage*: this is the period which gave rise to some of the world's greatest religious teachers and the formation of the world religions, as we know them. During this period religion becomes a great saving force with a strong doctrinal dimension. It was also during this period that people began to be taught religion as the old oral traditions gave way to the written word. The final stage is the current era, known as the *postaxial stage*. This stage is characterised by modernity and the fact that the world is (metaphorically speaking) a much smaller place. It is in this period that we are all much more aware of traditions different from our own. It also throws into sharp focus the problem of conflicting truth claims of religions which grew up during the axial stage. In the light of this some people think that is that in this new age we need to re-interpret what faith means.

Religion as the ultimate concern of humans

In this section we shall consider a particular definition of faith. The theologian Paul Tillich referred to religion as 'that which is of ultimate concern'.[7] This comment is very similar to the teacher who wanted to say that religion is 'Something which gives meaning to life'. We might also want to include under this heading the comments, 'Something which answers questions for people' and 'Looking after one's soul'. Essentially Tillich was writing about a particular understanding of what it means to be a human being. In Tillich's view what characterises humankind is the need to find meaning in life. James Fowler, the American psychologist, referred to this as human beings' need to 'construct an ultimate environment'.[8] Fowler, amongst others, referred to this human characteristic as faith.

Faith is a difficult word but an important one for RE teachers. One of the problems with the word is that nowadays people tend to equate the word *faith* with the word *belief* and use them as synonyms. So we talk about 'the Christian Faith', 'the Sikh Faith', etc, meaning 'the Christian religion', 'the Sikh religion'. In popular usage, to have faith in something can mean to believe in it; and this often means giving assent to a set of propositions or statements about the world. In one sense it is possible to say that faith has always been synonymous with belief. However, if we were to trace these words back in time we would find that believing meant much more than merely assenting to a set of statements about the world. St Anselm's famous statement 'Credo ut Intelligam' (I believe in order to understand)[9] does not refer to belief in this way. Rather it speaks of believing in terms of how we orientate ourselves. If we tell someone 'I believe in you,' we are not saying that 'I believe certain statements about you, you are 6 feet tall and slightly overweight'. We mean 'I trust you, I commit myself to you, I have faith in you.' Perhaps a better translation of Anselm's statement is 'I become involved in order to understand'.

In contrast to this, our modern understanding of belief is to do with the holding of certain ideas. Belief arises out of our efforts to interpret experiences into concepts and propositions. The word faith refers to something more personal. As we saw above, a religious person's search for meaning in life can be enriched, and their faith engendered, by the experience of worship and ritual of a particular religious tradition as well as the doctrines and teachings of the tradition. However, faith, and the person's search for meaning, do not lie in the religion but in the heart of the person. This is clearly described by Wilfred Cantwell-Smith when he writes that

> 'Prior to our being religious or irreligious, before we come to think of ourselves as Catholics, Protestants, Jews or Muslims, we are already engaged with issues of faith. Whether we become nonbelievers, agnostics or atheists, we are concerned with how to put our lives together and with what will make our life worth living. Moreover, we look for something to love that loves us, something to value that gives us value, something to honour and respect that has the power to sustain our being.'[10]

Therefore what we seem to be moving towards here is a distinction between the human desire for meaning and purpose, characterised by faith, and the religions which provide, for religious believers, the means to realise meaning in their lives. Of course people who are not religious believers find meaning in other ways whether it be political activity or football. So, according to this view, all of us, whether we call ourselves religious or not, are concerned with ultimate meaning. This in turn gives rise to what have come to be known as ultimate questions: questions such as 'What does it mean to live a good life?' 'What is happiness?' 'Why do the innocent suffer?' 'Who is my neighbour?' and so on. Such questions lie at the heart of religion and life in general. They help give the study of religion that spiritual dimension which disciplines such as sociology and history cannot. However, having said this, it must be emphasised that even though it seems that a characteristic of human nature is to seek meaning in life, and that not all human beings seek meaning in terms of religion, it is possible to say that there is such a thing as a religious meaning of life, and that any particular religion gives one set of interpretations of such a view.[11]

Religion as salvific

In the previous section we made a distinction between the human desire for meaning and purpose, characterised by faith, and the religions which provide, for religious believers, the means to realise meaning in their lives. It was a similar distinction to the one made by Eliade but with, perhaps, a greater optimism about the potential for modern human beings to live in a spiritual dimension.

In our search for an understanding of religion, we turn now to the idea that religion is about salvation. As Ninian Smart once said, the religions are, essentially, 'systems of Salvation'.[12] The scholar who has written most about this is John Hick.[13] Hick believes that attempts to define religion as a generic term are doomed to failure for the reasons we have already considered. Hick believes it is much better to study religions in their particularity and then describe them. In so doing we can then discover if they have anything in common. Religions are, according to Hick, like members of the same family, similar in many ways but not the same in all ways. For example, there may be similarities between Christianity and Buddhism. They share the concept of worship. However, worship does not mean the same in Christianity as it does in Buddhism, not least because Christians believe in God and for Buddhists God is not an important question.

According to Hick, the most important thing that religions have in common is that they provide an analysis of human unsatisfactoriness or incompleteness. Of course, for some religious believers their religion acts more as a form of identity. This aspect is important for RE but the really exciting and challenging thing about the religious traditions is that they provide a theory of human nature. If we apply this view to what we discussed in the previous section, we might say that the reason why humans need to search for meaning in their lives is because life in its natural state often seems ' nasty, brutish and short'.[14]

It is possible to identify key ideas, beliefs or concepts that express a particular religious tradition's analysis of human nature. Interestingly, whilst these concepts are different, they all point to the belief that there is something basically unsatisfactory or incomplete about being human. For a Christian, humans are incomplete because they are separated from God. That they are is due to the belief that humans are fallen creatures, a notion that is expressed in the story of Adam and Eve. For Muslims humans are incomplete because of *ghafala* (forgetfulness of Allah) and for Jews because of *yetzer ha-ra* (humans' innate inclination to do evil in a precarious life where survival is our pre-occupation). For Hindus, Sikhs, Jains and Buddhists the 'natural' human state is one of *avidya* (ignorance). Misguided by *maya* (illusion) humans are attached to *samsara* (the wearisome wheel of life, which is essentially unsatisfactory). For Buddhists such ignorance is the cause of *dukkha* (unsatisfactoriness) due to *tanha* (craving). For Sikhs it is *haumai* (human self-centredness).

However, according to this view, religions don't just provide an analysis of human nature but also provide a path, or way of living, which enables human beings to transcend this imperfect state and so enter a state which is believed to be more truly human. If we look at this in terms of the religious traditions, Hick's theory is emphasising that what is common between the religions is that they provide the means for humans to transcend incompleteness and so become more fully human. However, there is no attempt to say that the Buddhist view of human nature and destiny is the same as the Christian. For a Christian the path is one of redemption, found within the person of Jesus Christ, with the promise of eternal life. For the Buddhist, on the other hand, the eightfold path leads to *nibbana*. For the Hindu the path of non-attachment leads to *moksha*. For the Sikh it is the dual path of *nam simran* (God remembrance) and *sewa* (selfless service) which leads to a state of *anand* (bliss). The Muslim obedience to the will of Allah in terms of *Shariah* (divine law) and *tariqah* (the inward path) leads to paradise, and for the Jew atonement is reached by developing a right relationship with God by bringing *kedusha* (holiness) into the world.

On this analysis, then, religions could be described as ways which enable human beings to transcend their given, unsatisfactory, nature and achieve a state of being which is more spiritually advanced and, hence, ultimately more satisfying and rewarding.

Religion and religions

So far we have tended to use the terms 'religion' and 'religions' interchangeably. Does it matter, or is an attempt to discuss the possible difference in meaning between these two words merely the pedantic preoccupation of an ivory tower academic? I think it does matter, because what is decided here has implications about how we view our subject matter and, ultimately, how we teach.

If we look back at the previous sections we may be forgiven for concluding that there is such a thing as an essence of religion to which the different religions point. However, that would be to oversimplify what we have been saying. For what could this point be? We have seen that it can't be God. Perhaps the answer lies in Eliade's notion of the sacred? However Eliade seems to be describing a relationship between a particular type of human being and the world in which he or she inhabits. Religions have developed because of this relationship, but they are human constructs. Being human constructs, religions have a history and therefore change over time. By definition essences don't have a history and consequently don't change.

Thanks mainly to the work of Wilfred Cantwell Smith it is now widely accepted that the modern world has conferred names on religions where none previously existed. For example the words 'Hinduism' and 'Buddhism' are only about 200 years old and arose mainly because of a western desire to systemise and categorise. Even the word 'Christianity' did not exist before the Middle Ages. This tendency to form historical traditions into systems of belief has lead to the erroneous notion that, for example, all Hindus believe the same things and live their lives in the same way.

Smith's view is that when we talk about religion or religions we are describing the faith of human beings. For religious people this faith is defined in so far as they take part in the traditions of faith, what we call religions. We could go so far as to say that peoples' faith is formed and defined by the religious tradition to which they belong. But these traditions are not abstract systems but living traditions in which people are involved as individuals, as members of a family, as a community and so on. Moreover, faith is to be found in the human heart and not in the religion. Without the people there are no religions. This is summarised beautifully by Cantwell Smith in the following passage from his most famous book.

'Those of us on the outside who would interpret to ourselves the Muslim must understand not his religion but his religiousness. So for the Hindu, the Buddhist, the Tierra del Fuegin. If we would comprehend these we must look not at their religion but at the universe so far as possible through their eyes. It is what the Hindu is able to see, by being a Hindu, that is significant. Until we can see it too, we have not come to grips with the religious quality of his life. And we can be sure that when he looks around him he does not see 'Hinduism'. Like the rest of us, he sees his wife's death, his child's minor and major aspirations, his money lender's mercilessness, the calm of a starlight evening, his own mortality. He sees things through coloured glasses, if one will, of a 'Hindu' brand.[15]

In many respects this quotation brings us back to our teachers and their attempts to define what they understood religion to be. If you remember, our first attempt at coming to terms with this was to make a distinction between the statements 'Something that gives meaning to life' and 'Worship, rituals and celebrations'. We said that the former statement could be said to be an attempt at explaining religion generally in terms of why religion is important for people, and that it also hints at the spiritual significance of religion – that it gives life meaning. We then commented on the second statement, pointing out that it referred in a general sense to particulars which we associate with the phenomena of religion. As we know, each religion has its own particular forms of worship, ritual and celebration. We then suggested that it is the worship, rituals and celebrations that provide the means by which religious believers can find, as well as express, meaning.

In terms of the passage from Smith above, we can see how worship, ritual and celebrations, provide the 'coloured glasses' which the Hindu sees through in order to make sense of his life. Of course the 'coloured glasses' reflect more than just worship, ritual and celebration. They reflect also a whole string of concepts and ideas which help make sense of life and its ultimate questions. What our investigations have taught us, therefore, is that the importance of our attempts to understand religion is to see religion as something that enables human beings to see life in a certain way. While there may be no such thing as an essence of religion to which all religions point, there is, in a sense, an essence to being human. This essence is to do with human faith, in the way described by James Fowler. Therefore, what we have concluded is that to understand religion we have to attempt to understand the relationship between human faith, as described in this chapter, and how this faith is expressed in the various religious traditions of the world. In terms of RE this process has a personal dimension to it which, at its best, involves both pupils and teachers in an interactive and dialogical pedagogy. In the rest of this book we will be exploring some of the practical implications of this view.

[1] Marx, Karl *Contribution to the Critique of Hegel's Philosophy of Right*, 1844. The full quotation is, 'Religion is the sigh of the oppressed creature, the heart of a heartless world, just as it is the spirit of spiritless conditions. It is the opium of the people.'
[2] Otto, Rudolph, *The Idea of the Holy*, Penguin, 1959
[3] Eliade, Mircea, *The Sacred and the Profane*, Harcourt Brace and World, 1959
[4] Cantwell Smith, Wilfred, *The Meaning and End of Religion*, SPCK, 1978
[5] Bonhoeffer, Dietrich, *Letters and Papers from Prison*, SPCK, 1971
[6] Robinson, John, *Honest to God*, SCM, 1963
[7] Tillich, Paul, *The Shaking of the Foundations*, Penguin, 1962
[8] Fowler, James, *Stages of Faith: The Psychology of Human Development and the Quest for Meaning*, Harper and Row, 1981
[9] St. Anselm, *Proslogion*
[10] Cantwell Smith, Wilfred, *op. cit.*, p 5
[11] Ward, Keith, 'Religion and the Question of Meaning', in Joseph Runzo and Nancy Martin (eds), *The Meaning of Life in the World Religions*, One World, 2000
[12] Smart, Ninian, *The Phenomenon of Religion*, Macmillan, 1973
[13] Hick, John, *An Interpretation of Religion*, Macmillan, 1989
[14] Hobbes, Thomas, *Leviathan*, 1651. '(In a state of nature) No arts; no letters; no society; and which is worst of all, continual fear and danger of violent death; and the life of man, solitary, poor, nasty, brutish and short.
[15] Cantwell Smith, Wilfred, *op. cit.*, p 138

3 Process and planning in RE

Thinking about the process of RE

If you look at your local Agreed Syllabus you should be able to discern how the syllabus compilers view the process of learning in RE. One of the best places to look for this is in the syllabus's statement of aims for RE.

Most agreed syllabuses reflect a growing consensus about RE which places emphasis on three distinct but interrelated elements, which we briefly alluded to at the end of Chapter 1. It is very likely that, despite differences in wording, your syllabus advocates that RE should enable pupils to

- develop a knowledge and understanding of major religious traditions
- explore fundamental questions arising out of people's experience of life
- develop their own visions of life arising partly out of their studies.

Therefore the aims of recent agreed syllabuses indicate that successful planning and teaching of RE demands that these three elements of RE are integrated into a dynamic whole. In other words, our planning and teaching should enable our pupils to learn about religions in the light of questions about human experience, gain further insights into human living by applying their knowledge and understanding of religion to that experience, and learn from this exercise by being encouraged to develop their own beliefs and values.

Learning about *and learning* from *religion*

The QCA models of 1994 introduced teachers, inspectors and syllabus planners to these two concepts. In some agreed syllabuses, they formed two inter-related attainment targets. In actual fact, these two terms predate the QCA models by seven years. They were first introduced by Michael Grimmitt in his book *Religious Education and Human Development*.[1]

In practice, teachers have often found it difficult to make clear links between the two. While learning *about* religions seems straightforward enough, learning *from* religion has caused some problems. Many OFSTED inspectors refer to there being a lack of 'learning from' in RE lessons.

Of course, as we discovered in Chapter 2, there is a potential problem of confusion if the terms 'religions' and 'religion' are used interchangeably.

Therefore, does QCA's 'learning from' refer to learning from religions, or in using the term 'religion' do they mean something other than merely learning from aspects of the major religious traditions?

Recognising the difficulties which teachers have with the term 'learning from religion', QCA have published some guidance on this. According to QCA, learning from religion can be described as follows:

'Learning from religion is concerned with developing in pupils the capacity and skill to respond thoughtfully to and evaluate what they learn about religions.

Learning from religion allows pupils to make informed, reflective and personal responses based on their own experiences and values and engage with and interpret the views of others. They should interpret the significance of the data for themselves, for others, for their community and for the world. Pupils can do this in different ways and at different levels. Pupils can understand how believers in different religious traditions may interact with each other, not just historically but in contemporary ways, nationally and locally. Inter-faith issues can be explored.

Pupils should be able to make clear links between common human experiences and what religious people believe and do. Rituals, festivals, rites of passage, beliefs about God and the world – all these connect with common human experiences of awe, celebration, passage of time, a quest for meaning, purpose and value. Learning from religion requires pupils to see how such experiences are understood and interpreted in varying ways by members of different faiths and by those without religious beliefs. This plays a vital role in promoting pupils' spiritual, moral, social and cultural development.'[2]

The three-circle model for RE

Over the years, the staff at Westhill RE Centre in Birmingham have developed a three-circle model to represent the three elements of RE which we indicated at the beginning of this chapter.[3] One way of looking at the model is to see it as a map of the 'Field of Enquiry' of RE. If we look at it this way, then it is a model that describes the content of RE.

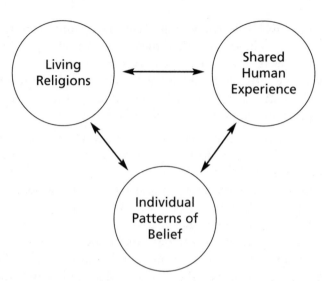

Figure 4: The content or 'field of enquiry' of RE

However, has we have seen so far, especially in Chapter 2, these are not three static pieces of knowledge from which we want pupils to learn. The content is actually a process. As we saw in Chapter 2, simply by being human we are inevitably engaged in a process. This is a key point to understanding the process of RE. It is possible to argue that one of the things about living in the west and inheriting the west's general understanding of religion is to approach religion in a way that can sometimes obscure from us the best ways of understanding it. Westerners tend to understand religion in terms of belief systems and religious believers as people who tend to believe things. This way of thinking is not always helpful to us if we really want to develop our understanding of the process of RE.

It is not that belief is unimportant, but more important to us as RE teachers is the way people, and especially but not exclusively religious people, 'see things'. We explored what this might mean with the example of the Hindu in Chapter 2. We also noted how James Fowler calls this way of seeing 'faith' which both he and Cantwell Smith distinguish from belief.

But the essential thing to grasp is that life and the religious life is a process. In terms of the model there is a dynamic interacting between the circles. In a sense, these circles are not separate at all.

It is this process from which we want pupils to learn. The model shown here seeks to illustrate the 'wholeness' of the process of RE. The model illustrates the three aspects as sources of content for RE but also describes the process of learning about and learning from as described here. Thus the process of RE should enable pupils to learn *about* religions (living faiths) in the light of questions about human experience (shared human experience), to gain further insights into human experience by applying their knowledge and understanding of religion to that experience, and to learn *from* this exercise by being encouraged to develop their own beliefs and values (individual patterns of belief). Any programme that fails to help children explore all three areas will in some way fail to achieve the overall aim for the subject.

Therefore this three-circle model is an attempt to describe something of this process of being human in a religious way and it is this process about which and from which we want pupils to learn. We can better describe the process of RE by representing the three circle model as follows:

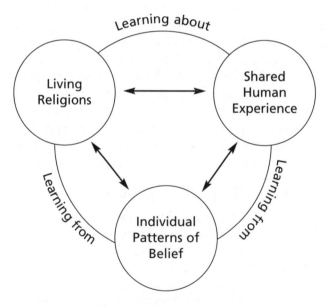

Figure 5: The process of RE

Thinking about planning RE topics

QCA schemes of work

By the time you are reading this book schools will have received the RE schemes of work from QCA. So the question arises, 'Do we need to think about planning if it has already been done for us?' Part of the answer to that question is probably no. It is difficult to imagine many busy primary teachers not taking advantage of this material, especially if they haven't got a very clear or detailed RE scheme of work already in place. However there are also good reasons for saying that it is still very important to think about planning. This is for two reasons. First, there are different approaches to planning and teaching RE, and a good knowledge of these different approaches will help you get the most out of the QCA schemes of work, if you choose to use them. Second, there is also the intention within the schemes that you plan your own topics sometimes. The schemes include some generic examples; for example Unit A2 (g) Worship and Community for Year 6. This topic is about exploring concepts such as worship and belonging. However, such an exploration can be achieved by using a variety of examples from religious traditions. This choice is left up to you. But how do you choose? What are the best examples to choose? What is your understanding of this type of approach to teaching RE? It is not a topic that just teaches children about an aspect of a particular religion but appears to be based on a variety of concepts. The following sections are intended to help you think through such questions and to equip you with the ability to plan your own topics and schemes.

Looking at the process of RE through questions

We have already noted that good planning and teaching of RE should seek to enable pupils to learn from all three areas of the field of enquiry. One way of ensuring that pupils have the opportunity to do this is to start to think about RE in terms of questions.

Good practice in RE should enable pupils to consider and reflect upon a variety of questions. Clarity about the types of questions we want our pupils to consider lies at the heart of good planning and teaching. It is possible to consider questions in terms of the three elements of RE. These three elements refer to each of the three circles in the model.

Element A: It is possible to say that a question such as 'How do Christians celebrate Easter?' is a question about a religion. Therefore we should be able to identify a list of questions under the first element (living religions) that are appropriate for pupils to learn about a particular religious tradition. Of course, it is important not to restrict such questions to 'What' and 'How' questions but to include some 'Why' questions. So it is not only important to consider what happens at an infant baptism, but also why Christian parents have their babies baptised.

Element B: However, there are other kinds of questions that are important for RE. A question such as 'Why do people suffer?' is not a question about a particular religion, but it is an important question for RE. It could be classed as a question about our shared human experience. That is, it is a question that, at one time or another, may concern any one of us simply because we are human beings. Moreover, those people who have a religious faith will try to make sense of such a question in the context of their faith. So, for example, a Buddhist will look to the teachings of Buddha on *Dukkha* (unsatisfactoriness) in order to try and make sense of the previous question. A Muslim may make sense of the question through his belief in *Qadar* (Allah's complete and final control over the fulfilment of events or destiny).

However, even those people who would not claim to be followers of a religious tradition are confronted with such questions. This is because these types of question are about matters of profound human concern and hence have a general dimension to them.

Element C: A third aspect of the process of RE is to enable pupils to apply a personal dimension (individual patterns of belief) to these general human questions; for example, 'What makes/would make me suffer?', or more particularly, 'Is there anything I can learn from what other people think about suffering and from how they deal with it?'

Good RE seeks to integrate these three elements and the questions which are characteristic of each. The three elements together form the basis for our understanding of what the content and process of RE should be about.

The figure on page 30 illustrates how appropriate questions can be identified using the Muslim tradition as an example. Notice how the questions under Elements B and C relate to the specific questions about the Muslim tradition in Element A.

Element A

Why do Muslims go on pilgrimage to Makkah?
How does a Muslim pray?
How do Muslims show their love for others?
What do Muslims celebrate?

Element B

Do we all need special places?
Does the world need prayers?
Is it important that people show love for others?
Why do people need to celebrate?

Element C

Have I a very special place?
Is prayer important to me?
How do I show love for others?
What and why do I celebrate?

Figure 6: Identifying appropriate questions in the context of the Muslim tradition

Of course it is not always possible or desirable to give equal prominence to each element in every RE topic we plan. This is one reason why it is important over a period of time to vary the way we plan RE topics units of work. We will deal with this in more detail in section 3 of this chapter.

Looking at the process of RE through concepts

Another aspect of good practice is to be able to decide in any given topic what ideas and concepts we wish our children to understand or begin to understand. This is vitally important because there is so much potential information we could include in RE. Pupils can't know everything there is to know, and if we fail to identify clearly what we want them to understand, we run the risk of overloading and confusing them with a plethora of knowledge.

What concepts do wish to help our pupils understand?

Again it is important to have the three elements of RE in mind. As we have noted, an important task of RE teaching is to enable pupils to make links between these three elements. A clear identification of specific concepts can help towards this. There are, essentially, three types of concepts from which we can draw to enable us to do this.

Concepts derived from the religions
Firstly, there are the concepts and ideas which belong within particular religious traditions and which relate to the key beliefs and values of each tradition. Potentially there are an enormous number of these and we have to be selective. The figure below identifies some key concepts belonging to each of the six major religious traditions (A glossary of these concepts is included at the end of the book.) We have chosen some essential concepts that anyone would need to be familiar with in order to be able to understand something of each tradition. This list is not exhaustive and for a much fuller list it is worth consulting the SCAA (QCA) Glossary of Terms.[4] Also some recent agreed syllabuses identify key concepts within the programme of study, or within examples of non-statutory guidance, so it is worth checking if your syllabus is one of those.

Buddhist	**Christian**	**Muslim**
Anatta	Church	Akhirah
Anicca	Discipleship	Allah
Buddha	Faith	Din
Dhamma	God the Father	Ibadah
Dukkha	Holy Spirit	Iman
Kamma	Jesus the Christ	Islam
Metta	Love	Jihad
Nibbana	Mother of God	Qadar
Sangha	Resurrection	Qur'an
Tanha	Salvation	Rasul
	Sin	Salah
Jewish	Trinity	Shari'ah
Brit		Shirk
Halakhah	**Hindu**	Sunnah
Israel	Ahimsa	Tawhid
Kashrut	Atman	Ummah
Mitzvah	Avatara	
Shabbat	Bhakti	**Sikh**
Shalom	Brahman	Anand
Synagogue	Dharma	Grace
Tenakh	Karma	Gurmukh
Teshuvah	Maya	Guru
Torah	Moksha	Haumai
Tzedekah	Samsara	Ik Onkar
	Shakti	Jivan Mukti
	Smriti	Khalsa
	Sruti	Nam Simran
	Varna	Sewa
	Yoga	Sikh

Figure 7: Concepts within the six major religious traditions (see Glossary)

Whatever the source of your concepts, it can be seen that in order that pupils develop an understanding of, say, Christianity, they will need to develop an understanding of concepts such as God the Father, Jesus the Christ, Holy Spirit, Church, salvation, etc. Likewise for Sikhism, they will need to develop an understanding of concepts like Guru, Anand, Seva, Sikh.

The kind of concepts discussed above relate specifically to what we have called Element A.

Concepts derived from human experience

It is also important to identify concepts from other areas if we are to enable pupils to enter fully into the process of RE. There are two other areas and the first relates specifically to what we have called Element B, shared human experience.

Examples of such concepts are listed in the figure (below) and, again, examples of such concepts may be found in some recent agreed syllabuses.

Service   Wonder   Guidance

Relationship   Teacher

Commitment   Suffering

Duty   Purity   Festival

Mystery   Authority   Unity   Care

Special place

Growth   Identity   Difference

Ritual

Celebration   Truth   Pattern   Community

Responsibility   Forgiveness

Belonging

Wholeness   Change

Leadership

Rule   Special time   Custom

Peace

Figure 8: Concepts derived from human experience

Although such concepts are not in themselves religious, they are very important in helping pupils make links between the three elements. They are the kind of concepts that we might refer to as 'spiritual' in that they help us make sense of significant aspects of our shared human experience. Such concepts are also related closely to the concepts of the religious traditions which are characteristic of Element A in the RE process.

Concepts derived from the study of religion
The third potential area from which we can select concepts for our planning does not relate specifically to any of the elements of RE but enables pupils to deal with religion in general. For example, an important task of RE teaching is to enable pupils to begin to understand something of the nature of religious language and communication. All religions communicate essential truths in non-literal ways. The frequency of poetic writings in sacred scripture is one example. Therefore, a concept such as myth is very important if pupils are to develop a sympathetic understanding of what sacred scripture is communicating to believers. Such a concept is also important because, like a number of concepts in this category, it has been devalued and reduced in meaning in many modern Western societies. The figure below lists some examples of this type of concept.

Fasting   Initiation   Pilgrimage

Belief   Religious tradition

Worship   Creation

Devotion

Prayer   God   Faith   Blessing

Symbol   Myth

Scripture

Figure 9: Concepts derived from the study of religion

Approaches to planning RE

Effective planning needs to take into account the three elements of RE. Over the years a number of approaches to planning RE have been developed. In this section we will look at three of them.

Planning based on a religious tradition (systems approach)

The systems approach[5] can be used to explore an aspect of a religious tradition in order to develop an understanding of that tradition. So for example, instead of trying to teach a class a topic called 'Hinduism' (an impossible task, especially in the primary school), a number of topics or units of work appropriate to the age of the pupils can be developed. For example, if we look at the QCA *Schemes of Work*, there is a topic or unit of work designed for Year 3 called 'How and why do Hindus celebrate Diwali?' there is also a unit, for Year 4, which builds on this and is called 'How do Hindus worship at home and in the mandir?' However, a systems approach effectively planned is not merely a means of passing on information about a particular religious tradition. If it is to be effective, in terms of the process of RE, a systems approach needs to take all three elements of RE into account. To see how this can be done look at the

Celebrating Diwali: Year 3		
Key questions	*Key concepts*	*Possible content drawn from Hinduism*
How do Hindus celebrate Diwali? Why do Hindus celebrate Diwali? Why do we celebrate? What do we celebrate? Who do we celebrate with? What things in life are good and evil? Can good overcome evil?	Rama the *avatara* Light Celebration Symbol Goodness Evil	How Diwali is celebrated in the home and in the temple Story of Rama and Sita Rama as *avatara* of Vishnu

Figure 10: Outline of a systems approach

questions and concepts in the Diwali example below. In the systems approach the main emphasis tends to be on the first element, living religions. However, the concepts are drawn from Hinduism (*avatara*, in this case Rama), human experience (celebration) and the study of religion (symbol). The idea is that in learning something about an aspect of Hinduism, pupils are also enabled to learn from this topic by applying their knowledge of Hinduism to questions about life, their own life concerns, and their understanding of religion in general.

Planning using a cross-religions approach

Planning using a cross-religions approach has proved very popular over the years. In this approach material is drawn from a number of religions in order to illustrate a theme. Originally its origins lay in the work of Ninian Smart.[6] Using a method called phenomenology, Smart studied religion in its many forms and concluded that they can all be studied in seven dimensions. These dimensions are:

- rituals (services, festivals, ceremonies)
- narratives and myths (scriptures, stories)
- doctrines and philosophies (creeds, statements of faith)
- ethics (guidance on moral, social and environmental issues)
- social institutions (for example the church in Christianity, the Sangha in Buddhism but also the vision that each religion provides for an ideal society)
- a material dimension (buildings and works of art)
- an experiential dimension.

In a very real sense it is the last, experiential, dimension that lies at the core of all the others. It concerns the emotions and experience of religious believers, and it is what motivates them and gives meaning to rituals, creeds and ethical demands. This dimension of religious experience is what gives religion a unity. Smart maintained that it is possible to study the dimensions separately, but they are all part of the whole of religious experience.

We mentioned in Chapter 1 how Smart's work influenced the implicit and explicit approaches to RE. Explicit RE often took the form, and still does, of cross-religions themes. So for example, festivals, sacred scriptures, founders of religions, worship, to give just a few examples, can be studied deriving content from a number of religious traditions because they all share these dimensions. Unfortunately, in practice, some aspects of this approach have done a disservice to RE. This kind of cross-religions thematic approach has been highly criticised in some quarters[7] for confusing children, not respecting the distinctiveness and integrity of individual religions, concentrating on the peripheries of religion and, consequently, failing to engage pupils with the spiritual dimension. In some cases such criticisms are fair and appropriate.

I recently visited a school where Year 4 pupils were following a theme on festivals called 'Spring Festivals'. Ironically this was a school where the RE was of a high standard, but there was something wrong with 'Spring Festivals'. The theme drew its content from the three Semitic traditions, Judaism, Christianity and Islam. One festival from each was the focus of study. From Judaism it was Passover (or Pesach) because it falls in the month of Nisan which occurs in the spring. From Christianity it was Easter, and from Islam it was Ramadan. Leaving aside the question as to whether or not Ramadan can be classed as a festival (it would be more accurate to include Eid-ul-Fitr, which occurs as a celebration at the end of Ramadan), Ramadan does not necessarily occur in the spring. In 1999 it took place in December and January. Muslims follow a lunar calendar and so the date of Ramadan changes year by year.

This unfortunate mishmash of religious festivals appears to fall prey to most of the criticisms of a cross-religions approach. First, it does not do justice to the distinctiveness of the traditions because it misrepresents one of them. Second, because of that, it cannot help but confuse pupils, especially Muslim pupils! Third by tying together these festivals under the heading of 'Spring Festivals' there is a danger of concentrating on the peripheries and therefore failing to engage pupils with the spirituality of these traditions. It is true that Easter and Passover occur in spring but, apart from being symbolic of new life or new beginnings, spring is incidental to the true meaning of these festivals.

Other critics may find fault with themes such as 'Founders of Religions'. Muslims would point out that it is a sin (*shirk*) to refer to Muhammad as the founder of Islam. That would be to place inappropriate importance on the prophet, who while being the perfect example of a human being for Muslims is, nevertheless, not God. For Muslims there is only one religion, the religion of submission to Allah, which is what 'islam' means. Islam was a concept long before it was a label. It is interesting to note that this kind of confusion is partly the result of the kind of issues we were discussing in Chapter 2. It is to do with westerners viewing religion in terms of separate belief systems and consequently confusing the concept 'islam' with the label Islam. The concept islam refers to all true believers who are called muslims. There have always been muslims and the first prophet of islam was Adam. But if there is a founder of Islam it is God not man! The kind of cross-religions themes, such as those described here, do not only present Islam inaccurately. It is difficult to see Jesus as the founder of Christianity, for example. True, the Christian tradition begins with Jesus but to concentrate on Jesus as the founder of anything rather than the reformer of his inherited tradition, Judaism, is to miss the point.

Also, what many of us take to be the identity of Sikhs, namely the wearing of the 5 K's, actually began with the tenth Guru, Guru Gobin Singh, although the spiritual tradition does lie with the teachings of Guru Nanak.

Does this mean, therefore, that it is unwise to plan RE using a cross-religions theme approach? If it is, then QCA have been unwise. In the primary RE schemes of work there are several examples of cross-religions themes such as Worship and Community, Why are sacred texts important?, and How do people express their faith through the arts?, in Year 6. There is also a topic called, What are Harvest Festivals?, for Year 1.

Despite what the critics say, it is possible to plan RE using a cross-religions approach with integrity. But how can we make sure that cross-religions themes do not present the kind of problems described above? The answer lies on pages 31-33 of this book. There we looked at three different categories of concepts. The first category was concepts derived from specific religions. The second category was concepts derived from human experience; and thirdly, there was the category derived from the study of religion. It is this third category that should underpin any attempt to plan using a cross-religions approach. This is because concepts such as 'worship' and 'scripture' do cut across the various religions. Christian worship may be different from Sikh worship but the Sikhs and Christians do share the practice and belief in the importance of worship. Therefore it is possible to explore the meaning of worship and broaden our understanding of the concept by looking at worship in different traditions. Moreover, it is possible to argue that in this respect RE plays a significant role in developing pupils' understanding of religion as a whole.

It is rather more difficult with a theme like festivals. This is because 'festivals' does not really fit into the category of concepts illustrated on pages 31-33. It is probably better to emphasise the concept of 'celebration' and remember that festivals celebrate different things. Some festivals for example celebrate and recall past events which are significant within the tradition. Examples would be the importance of the Exodus story for Jews celebrating Passover or the story of the founding of the Sikh Khalsa at Baisakhi. It might in such cases be better to explore these examples as part of a systems approach to Judaism and Sikhism. In terms of festivals and cross-religions themes it might be better to concentrate on ways of celebrating such as celebrating with light or food. While not without their dangers the concept of symbolism can be highlighted and thus give the theme more conceptual coherence.

In conclusion, therefore, cross-religions themes have their part to play in a balanced programme of religious education, but effective planning requires conceptual clarity. If in doubt, think about the process of RE as described in this book. Think about how planning can best enable pupils to learn about and from religion in a way that respects the nature of individual religions, adds to pupils' understanding by not confusing them, and enables them to learn something about the spirituality of religion.

Planning using a human experience approach

Planning using a human experience approach derives its focus from the second element of the process of RE and seeks to emphasise the questions and concepts associated with this element. It differs from the cross-religions approach in that it seeks to explore that which is common to humans as they experience the world, irrespective of whether they interpret that experience within the context of a religious tradition or not. Writers such as Fowler, with his broad definition of faith, could be said to have influenced this approach. We noted in Chapter 2 that Fowler referred to faith as being about the human need to 'construct an ultimate environment'. In other words simply by being human we are involved with the 'big' questions of existence such as 'Why are we here?' 'What is our destiny?', 'Who is my neighbour?', 'Why do humans have to suffer?' and so on. It is these 'ultimate' questions which provide the basis for the human experience approach to planning and teaching RE.

The idea of this approach is that pupils explore a particular issue or question about life, such as 'Who is my neighbour'. This question is then explored within the context of content drawn from a number of religious traditions. Initially we would want the pupils to consider this question from their own experience by exploring, for example, what they understand the term 'neighbour' to mean, based on their short experience of life. Is it just the person who lives next door, or does it refer to a wider group of people? Teachers would probably develop this by reading stories. In terms of content drawn from the religious traditions it would be possible, for example, to visit or invite into school a representative of the Salvation Army so that they could talk about their work. This would enable the pupils to understand something about the Christian concept of charity. In addition to this the class might visit a Sikh Gurdwara and enjoy a snack and a glass of coke in the langar. This traditional form of Sikh hospitality will introduce the pupils to the Sikh concept of *sewa* (selfless service). In this way the theme is planned to broaden and deepen the pupils understanding of 'who is a neighbour'. The focus is not on an attempt to enable the pupils to 'understand Christianity or Sikhism': this is what the systems approach is better suited for. The idea is to expand their experience of the world and to appreciate something about our commonality as humans and our need for love and neighbourliness. This theme then is an attempt to enable pupils to learn more about human relationships.

Even though the focus is on human experience rather than the religions, this approach is similar to all others in as much as key questions and concepts need to be identified, but unlike the systems approach concepts and content should be drawn from more than one religious tradition. The example below may make this clearer.

Topic: Loving and Giving: Who is my neighbour?		
Key questions	*Key concepts*	*Possible content drawn from Christianity and Sikhism*
How can we show someone we love them? How do we know when someone loves us? When is it easy or difficult to show love? Should we only love those we know? How do Christians and Sikhs show love?	Relationships Care Love Charity (Christian) Sewa (Sikh)	Stories from New Testament and Janam Sakhi (life stories of Guru Nanak) Christan groups who care (eg The Salvation Army) Visit to a Sikh Gurdwara to learn about sewa

Figure 11: Outline of a human experience approach. A fully worked out example of this is included in Chapter 4

Human relationships is just one category that might be explored using a human experience approach to planning. The table overleaf gives some others with some ideas for topic titles within each category.

Categories of human experience	Potential areas for raising ultimate questions and sample topic headings
The natural world	Human awareness of the world around us – the orderliness of nature, the regularity of seasons, resources for food, energy and wealth; the awe-inspiring aspects – natural wonders and disasters, power of natural forces, the interrelatedness of all living things, the vastness of the universe and details of the microcosm, the origins and future of the earth, the natural life cycle. Topic examples: KS1 Looking after the Earth; KS 2 'Why are we here?'
Relationships	Relationships of family and enmity, both personal and social; the family and relationships within the family; belonging to groups based on interest, cause or belief; relationships of equality, superiority or inferiority; personal, familial, social and national identity. Topic examples: KS1 Learning from others; KS2 'Who is my neighbour?'
Rules and issues	The rules by which people live; codes of behaviour; legal and moral rules; personal and social moral issues such as war and peace, inequality, human rights, poverty and affluence, law and order, euthanasia and abortion, the environment, democracy. Topic examples: KS1 Rules about what we eat and drink; KS2 Rules of the group
Stages of life	The human life process and the changes in outlook that growth and decay bring; experiences associated with childbirth, maturation, old age and death; rites of passage, particularly those associated with birth, initiation, marriage and death. Topic examples: KS1 Beginnings; KS2 Life's journey
Celebrations	Ceremonies which mark important occasions in personal and community life – birthdays, anniversaries, festivals, fasts and solemn days; community national and religious occasions; celebrations of events, people and values. Topic examples: KS1 Celebrating special days; KS2 Celebrating with light

continued

Lifestyles	The way of living that people adopt as an expression of their identity, belief or culture – customs of food and clothing; communal, regimented and independent lifestyles, monastic and ascetic patterns of living; competitive and cooperative lifestyles, lifestyles which represent a non-conformist reaction to current norms, eg vegetarianism.
	Topic examples: KS1 Families; KS2 'What I would like to be and do'
Suffering	Human suffering as a result of disease, natural disasters, accidents; suffering as a result of war, violence and other conflict; cruelty to other human beings and animals; persecution, racial discrimination and oppression in any form; the Holocaust; human responses to the problems of evil and suffering.
	Topic examples: KS1 Losing things that are precious; KS2 'Do all things come to an end?'

Figure 12: Categories of human experience

It is significant that the QCA schemes of work do not include any examples of planning in this way. It is interesting to speculate as to why this is. As we mentioned during our discussion of cross-religions themes, there has been some recent controversy about thematic teaching in RE.[8] However, it would seem an unfortunate outcome of this controversy if the teaching profession was to lose its nerve and consign a legitimate and effective approach to the educational dustbin.

Another reason for the current lack of popularity of this approach may rest in the current craze, amongst politicians at least, on the acquisition of knowledge. Indeed it is possible to argue that the appearance of the QCA model syllabuses for RE in 1994 pushed the subject down a very content/knowledge orientated route. Even though the model syllabuses were no more than guidelines and did not prescribe content, they have, arguably, had a considerable influence on schools which have been forced, possibly out of fear of doing wrong, to concentrate on knowledge-based schemes of work.

There are probably two other reasons for the apparent neglect of this way of planning and teaching RE. Of the three approaches discussed here it is perhaps the most demanding on the teacher. While all approaches should reflect the process of RE, the human experience approach demands that the teacher really understands this process; that she really does understand Cantwell-Smith's words (see page 22) or James Fowler's theory of faith development. Also it demands that the teacher knows quite a lot about the different religious traditions. A final reason for neglect is probably connected with assessment. A teacher recently asked me, 'How can one measure children's spiritual and moral development?' Leaving aside whether it is wise to use the terms 'measure' and 'spiritual development' in the same sentence, it would be fair to say that many primary teachers have felt more comfortable with the knowing and understanding aspects of RE. This is particularly the case when teachers are asked to assess pupils' progress in the subject. Whether or not assessment in RE demands we only focus on knowledge and understanding we shall explore in Chapter 4.

[1] Grimmitt, Michael, *Religious Education and Human Development*, McCrimmon, 1987

[2] QCA, *Non-statutory guidance on RE*, Qualifications and Curriculum Authority, 2000

[3] Read, Garth *et al*, *How do I Teach RE?* second edition, Westhill RE Centre, 1998. Teece, Geoff, *How to Write Your Scheme of Work for RE*, Westhill RE Centre, 1996. QCA, *op. cit.*, pages 21-22. All three of these sources give more detail on the systems approach. The recent QCA document helpfully distinguishes approaches that begin with a concept derived from a religious tradition and those that begin with the experience of a member of a religious tradition. This latter approach has been called the 'ethnographic' approach. A full rationale for this can be found in Jackson, Robert, *Religious Education: an interpretive approach*, Hodder and Stoughton 1997

[4] The SCAA Glossary of Terms should be available in your school. If not contact QCA or visit their website, www.qca.org.uk

[5] For a full exposition of the systems approach see *How do I Teach RE*, pages 40-47

[6] Smart, Ninian, *The World's Religions*, second edition Cambridge 1998

[7] See for example, Burn, John and Hart, Colin, *The Crisis in Religious Education*, The Educational Research Trust 1988

[8] Teece, Geoff, *In Defence of Theme Teaching in Religious Education*, Westhill RE Centre, 1993

4 Assessment

The purpose and principles of assessment

The area of RE that causes most concern for teachers is probably assessment. There are several reasons for this. There are no statutory requirements as in the core subjects of the National Curriculum. There is no National Curriculum in RE, so advice and practice vary from local authority to local authority and Agreed Syllabus to Agreed Syllabus. And there is doubt in some teachers' minds as to whether we can or should assess pupils' progress and attainment in RE at all. The kind of concerns are highlighted in the two following examples, both expressed on a recent course about assessment in RE. As mentioned at the end of Chapter 3, one member of the group raised the question, 'How can one assess the spiritual and moral development of pupils?' Another teacher bemoaned the lack of support from her head in allowing her time and resources to develop assessment in the school. The headteacher's reply to her concerns was 'We can't assess God!' It is an interesting reply given that the school was about to undergo an inspection in which it would be expected that there would be policies and arrangements for assessment.

What these two examples illustrate is a confusion in teachers' minds about RE and where it fits in the current curriculum and educational environment that stresses accountability, objective assessments, league tables and so on. There is an implicit concern in the first question mentioned above that somehow RE doesn't fit in with all these developments, that the integrity of the subject will somehow be compromised by going down the assessment route.

There is a twofold response to this. First, it depends on what mean by assessment. Second, although RE is perhaps different in some ways from other subjects, it is like other subjects in that we need to be able to set out what we are trying to achieve, what the pupils should be learning and how we are going to find out about their progress.

What kinds of assessment?

Perhaps part of the problem is that many people have too narrow a view of what assessment is. Despite the great progress made in thinking about assessment, the current emphasis on SATs and league tables, and its consequent anxieties, has over-emphasised a narrow, summative view of assessment. However, many teachers appreciate that there are three main purposes of assessment. These are described below.

What is assessment for?

- *Identifying pupils' strengths and weaknesses*
  This is diagnostic assessment. This kind of assessment involves setting pupils tests to assist us in our planning. An example of this is an audit of knowledge. For example we might want to know how much our class knows about Christianity before we plan an introductory topic to the religion. The results of diagnostic assessments are not shared with the pupils but enable teachers to plan better to meet pupils' needs.

- *Assisting pupils in their learning*
  This is formative assessment. This kind of assessment involves making regular and continual judgements about pupils' progress. The results are shared with pupils because the purpose is to help them to learn.

- *Identifying achievement based on stated criteria*
  This is summative assessment. This means making overall judgements at the end of a period of teaching and learning for the purpose of reporting pupils' achievement. These assessments are for the benefit of 'outside agencies' such as parents and employers.

Figure 13: What is assessment for?

What are we trying to assess in RE?

Any discussion of this question must be related to our understanding of the process of RE. In an effort to make this discussion understandable to all teachers, recent developments in RE have seen this process described in terms of two attainment targets, Attainment Target 1: 'Learning about religion and human experience' and Attainment Target 2: 'Learning from religion and human experience'. Some agreed syllabuses may use the terms contained in the QCA models 'Learning about religions' and 'Learning from religion'. It would be tempting to say that this difference is only one of semantics. Nevertheless for reasons explored in Chapters 2 and 3, in this book we prefer the former because in our view 'learning about and from religion and human experience' better describes the process of RE than the QCA terms. In many agreed syllabuses, these two attainment targets indicate the areas of RE in which pupils' progress and achievements can be assessed. It should also be recognised that not all aspects of teaching and learning in RE are assessable. Some would want to add that there are also some areas that should not be assessed. Two examples of this might be personal matters that pupils wish to keep to themselves, and making judgements as to whether pupils' beliefs and values are right or wrong. Of course such issues may well form part of discussion in RE but they are not matters to be assessed.

As we noted at the beginning of this chapter, one of the problems with assessment in RE has been the variety of approaches taken in different agreed syllabuses. Not only has there been, until recently, different attainment targets, there have also been differences in the assessment arrangements themselves. RE has always had an uneasy relationship with the rest of curriculum in this respect. Should RE have levels of attainment or end of key stage statements or descriptors? If we were to examine a selection of agreed syllabuses we would find all three! Some would say the local automony of RE enables providers, in theory, to resist national developments of which they disapprove. Others would disagree, pointing out that RE needs national guidance on what we should be expecting of pupils. For example, Ofsted inspections have regularly shown that assessment in RE is generally weak.

Consequently, QCA in association with AREIAC (The Association of RE Advisers, Inspectors and Consultants), has recently published guidelines for agreed syllabus conferences that set out a nine-point scale of expectations in RE.[1]

This is not the place to enter a debate as to whether or not RE should 'go national'. What is more important, for our purposes, is to say that whatever the expectations and requirements are, effective assessment is dependent on effective planning.

Planning and assessment

If we want to be effective in our assessments of pupils' progress then we need to be clear about what we want our pupils to learn in RE. In Chapter 3 we considered the kinds of questions we want pupils to raise, and concepts we want them to understand. Identification of appropriate questions and concepts that are derived from religion and human experience is essential both to effective teaching and effective assessment.

There are, however, two other elements of learning that we need to consider when planning for assessment. These two elements are the identification of appropriate skills and attitudes.

Attitudes in RE

It would be wrong to think that RE has a monopoly on promoting certain attitudes. It is important for learning in general that pupils develop appropriate attitudes. Nevertheless there are attitudes that are fundamental to the development of learning in RE. While understanding in general has a personal, attitudinal dimension, understanding in RE often involves the understanding of people and why people behave as they do, believe what they believe, and are as they are. To understand these sorts of things requires the adopting of certain attitudes. A selection of these is given in the table below.

Attitudes in RE

- A sensitivity towards the environment
- A willingness to acknowledge the needs, feelings and aspirations of others
- Respect for others, and a willingness to learn from them
- Respect for the freedom to practise or not to practise religion
- A willingness to accept that beliefs and ideas may be expressed in a variety of ways
- A willingness to acknowledge the controversial and ambiguous nature of many issues about life
- Confidence in one's sense of identity
- A willingness to value diversity in religion and culture

Figure 14: Attitudes in RE

Skills in RE

It is generally agreed that there are no skills peculiar to RE. However, there are some important skills in which we should require pupils to develop so that they can develop the kinds of concepts and attitudes that RE requires. It might be helpful to think about skills in relation to different categories related to the process of RE. Some examples are given in the table opposite.

Skills in RE

Skills needed to explore religion and human experience
- Investigating
- Questioning
- Observing
- Listening
- Researching

Skills needed to understand religion and human experience
- Reflecting
- Imagining
- Interpreting
- Empathising
- Analysing
- Synthesising

Skills needed for personal response
- Expressing
- Communicating
- Concluding
- Valuing
- Evaluating

Figure 15: Skills in RE

The identification of appropriate concepts, skills and attitudes forms the basis for clarity in planning, effectiveness in teaching and realistic expectations in assessment.

Let us see how this can work in practice. Included below are two 'mid-term' units of work, or RE topics. These are written for Year 2 and Year 6. These units have been deliberately planned using a thematic, human experience approach. One reason for doing this is that teachers often find it relatively easy to think about assessment in terms of knowledge and understanding or learning *about* religion, but they find thinking about assessment in terms of learning *from* religion a lot more problematical. If you look at the units you can see the kinds of questions, concepts, skills and attitudes that have been identified for each topic. There is also an indication of content derived from the Agreed Syllabus programme of study, as well as a series of activities that are designed to enable the pupils to meet the learning objectives which are identified in the first column under the title 'attainment focus'. These learning objectives are based on the assessment requirements of two different agreed syllabuses. As such requirements and the writing of objectives are crucial to effective assessment, we shall now look at them in more detail.

Using an end of key stage descriptions approach

The year 6 example, 'Why are we here?' is written in accordance with the assessment arrangements of the Birmingham Agreed Syllabus (see Figure 17). This syllabus was published in 1995 and developed the end of key stage approach. Those who support this approach will say that it lightens the assessment load and provides a more flexible means of assessment than the tighter structure of levels. They would also point to the difficulty of measuring pupil progress in terms of levels, especially in terms of the more personal, responsive, aspect of RE. People's spiritual development does not develop in an orderly, fixed, incremental kind of way that 'levels' suggest. Nevertheless some would argue that end of key stage descriptions are not very helpful to teachers trying to assess pupils who are not at the end of a key stage; for example, how does a description for a Year 6 pupil related to a pupil in Year 4?

Using a steps or levels approach

The Year 2 example, 'Loving and Giving', is written in accordance with the assessment arrangements of the Staffordshire Agreed Syllabus. (See Figure 19). Staffordshire has developed a 'steps' approach based on an eight level scale that parallels the levels of the National Curriculum with a level nine for exceptional performance at Key Stage 4 and in the sixth form. The work being developed at QCA, mentioned above, is similar to this.

These steps are broad statements of progress and would need to be revisited several times before assigning a particular level to a particular pupil. The steps are also designed to help teachers write effective objectives for their mid and short term planning.

The importance of objectives

Indeed, whatever approach is taken, be it end of key stage descriptions or levels, teachers need to be able to frame clear and achievable learning objectives if effective assessment is to take place. So, for example, if we look at the first column (attainment focus) of each of the two units, we can see that an example objective or indicator has been included. This helps focus the level or description from the Agreed Syllabus so that it relates specifically to the intended learning outcomes of the specific topic. Some would want to argue that each level or description needs more than one objective in order to account for differentiation. This is an important point. To give an example: for the AT1 description *Understand some of the beliefs and values of religious traditions* in the topic 'Why are we here?', we might want an objective that requires pupils to retell the stories of creation. This would be a lower level objective when compared to the one included, which expects pupils to explain the meaning of the stories. By using the two we are in a better position to be able to say something about the attainment of all the pupils in the class. Of course, in some cases two objectives will not be enough and a third might need to be added. The QCA schemes of work are very helpful in this respect. For each unit of work there is a section headed 'Expectations'. This section advises the teacher that at the end of the particular unit of work,

- Most children will ...
- Some children will not have made so much progress and will ...
- Some children will have progressed further and will ... .

So these example schemes allow the teacher to use three different levels of response to the topic in question.

This is helpful because teachers don't necessarily find writing objectives for RE very easy. Some agreed syllabuses are helpful in that they give some example objectives or indicators related to the levels or descriptions. The table below is intended to help with the writing of objectives for RE. When writing learning objectives it is useful to have a bank of expressions that help you express clear statements. These expressions often relate to the skills that we want pupils to develop.

Year Group 6	Term: Autumn	Teaching Time c 6/7 hrs
Attainment focus	Questions and concepts	Syllabus content
AT2 – Learning from Religion **Questioning (EKSD)** • *Raise questions about beliefs and values ...* So that they could, for example, • Express their own beliefs and values about creation **Applying (EKSD)** • *Consider the implications of their own beliefs and values for themselves and others* So that they could, for example, • Make judgements about the relationship between humans and the natural world **AT1 – Learning about Religion (EKSD)** • *Understand some of the beliefs and values of religious traditions* So that they could, for example, • Explain the meaning for believers of the two creation stories	**Questions** • Why are we here? • Who made us? • Who made the world? • What are our repsonsibilities towards the world? **Concepts** • Creation • Responsibility • Care • Mystery • God • Brahma • Stewardship	**AT2** • *Dinosaurs and all that Rubbish* • Reflection upon their own thoughts, feelings and experiences and express through a variety of media • Compare and contrast their own viewpoints with those learned from the studied religions **AT1** • Creation stories from Genesis • Hindu creation story: The First World

Figure 16: Unit of Work for Year 6 – Why are we here?

Unit title: Why are we here?

Teaching/learning activities	Assessment focus	Resources
• Discussion about different types of questions using formative assessment sheet • Group focussed discussion on the question 'Why are we here?' • Reading and discussion of *Dinosaurs* and Genesis 1. Discussion of issues arising out of stories • Group activities enabling pupils to interpret creation for themselves using a variety of media (music, art, drama etc) • Read 'First World' Hindu story of creation • Express the story through dance • Compare and contrast the two creation stories looking for common themes • Discussion leading to practical care of environment	• **Formative assessment** (Why are we here?) • **Summative assessment** Writing of poem Skills/attitudes • Questioning • Reflecting • Imagining • Expressing • Valuing • Exercising judgement • Sensitivity to the living and non living environment	• Copies of Biblical story 'The First World' from *A Tapestry of Tales* • Worksheets • Art materials • Musical instruments

End of Key Stage Descriptions for Religious Education

An indication of what pupils should be achieving by the end of each Key Stage

	Key Stage One by age 7, pupils should:	Key Stage Two by age 11, pupils should:
Learning about Religion Knowing and understanding	be aware that there are aspects of their own and other people's lives that are especially important to them *so that they could, for example:* talk about occasions, places or people in a way which shows that they are particularly special.	recongnise that people's actions may signify what is important to them *so that they could, for example:* describe how Muslim prayer expresses a relationship with God.
Learning from Religion Questioning	be aware that there are many questions about the mystery of life that are very challenging *so that they could, for example:* ask questions such as, 'Why are there people?'	recognise that questions they raise about beliefs and values may give rise to a variety of answers *so that they could, for example:* recognise that, when they ask questions such as 'Is there life after death?' people may give different answers.
Evaluating	be able to express their own feelings, reactions and responses in creative ways *so that they could, for example:* draw a picture showing what they found interesting in their visit to a local place of worship.	be able to express a sensitive personal opinion about issues of belief and value *so that they could, for example:* give their own opinion about vegetarianism while showing they have considered other points of view.
Applying	recognise possible connections between their own and other people's experiences *so that they could, for example:* talk about their own experiences of special places when visiting a place of worship.	be able to describe similarities and differences between their own and other people's experiences *so that they could, for example:* contrast the experience of making an important journey with a believer's experience of going on a pilgrimage.

Figure 17: Birmingham Agreed Syllabus – End of Key Stage Descriptions

Key Stage Three by age 14, pupils should:	Key Stage Four by age 16, pupils should:
understand some of the beliefs and traditions of particular religious traditions *so that they could, for example:* explain what Christians mean by calling Jesus 'Lord'.	understand ways in which people apply their beliefs and values to contemporary situations and issues *so that they could, for example:* discuss how belief in stewardship affects people's attitudes to the environment.
raise questions about beliefs and values which may arise from particular situations *so that they could, for example:* be able to show how a natural disaster can prompt questions such as 'Why do innocent people suffer?'	understand that, in the questions they raise, there are differences between questions of belief and value, and other kinds of questions *so that they could, for example:* explain differences between questions such as 'How does the human body work?' and questions such as 'Do we have souls?'
be able to give a reasoned viewpoint of their own in response to issues about beliefs and values *so that they could, for example:* explain whey they agree/disagree with the view that everything in life is already decided.	be able to present a thoughtful personal response to questions and issues about beliefs and values, taking sensitive account of views different from their own *so that they could, for example:* give a balanced statement of their own view on the 'right to die' issue, taking account of different viewpoints.
consider the implications of their own beliefs and values for themselves and others *so that they could, for example:* describe how the view 'charity begins at home' might apply to themselves and others.	consider the relevance of the beliefs and values of others to their own outlook and way of life *so that they could, for example:* show how their own viewpoint about reincarnation has been influenced by the views of other people.

Year Group 2	Term: Spring	Teaching Time c 6/7 hrs
Attainment focus	Questions and concepts	Syllabus content
AT2 – Lifestance • *Express their own ideas of what is of value and concern to them* So that they could, for example, • Talk about how people show love to them **AT2 – Issues** • *Show some awareness of people's values ...* So that they could, for example, • Explain why people believe it is important to show loving behaviour towards others **AT1 – Religion** • *Describe some religious practices ...* So that they could, for example, • Explain how Christians and Sikhs show love **AT1 – Meaning** • *Suggest and begin to identify meanings behind religious imagery ...* So that they could, for example, • Explain the meaning of the Good Samaritan	**Questions** • How can we show someone we love them? • How do we know when someone loves us? • When is it easy or difficult to show love? • Should we only love those we know? • How do Christians and Sikhs show love? **Concepts** • Relationships • Care • Love • Charity (Christian) • Sewa (Sikh)	**AT2** • Stories: Shirley Hughes *Giving*, Jenny Wagner *John Brown Rose and the Midnight Cat* • Children's own examples of loving behaviour • Discussions on how we can show love • Compare and contrast own viewpoints with those learned from the religions studied **AT1** • Stories from Christianity (eg The Good Samaritan) and Sikhism (Janam Sakhies) • Christian groups who care (eg The Salvation Army) • Visit to a Sikh Gurdwara to learn about sewa

Figure 18: Units of Work for Year 2 – Loving and Giving

Unit title: Loving and Giving

Teaching/learning activities	Assessment focus	Resources
• Children to bring in photographs of people who love them or who they love • Discussion on how people show love (eg presents, hugging, celebrations) • Read and discuss the story of the Good Samaritan • Children do worksheet showing some people helping others and some not. Children to colour in or circle those pictures showing loving behaviour • Invite a Salvation Army Officer to come in and talk about her work • Read the Sikh story *A Good Bargain* • Visit a Sikh Gurdwara and have lunch in the langar • Involve the class in a fund-raising project sush as Children's Society, Christian Aid, Sikh Cultural Society	• **Formative assessment** After discussion make a class list of the different ways in which people show love *or* Use the worksheet (see activities) • **Summative Assessment** Write an account of the story of the Good Samaritan Skills/attitudes • Valuing • Empathising • Reflecting • Expressing • Communicating • Listening • Have confidence in their own sense of identity • Show a willingness to recognise the needs and feelings of others	• Stories • Large format pictures • Artefacts

Learning about Religion

Steps	Religion *Exploring and understanding religious beliefs and practices and their influence on society* Pupils can:	Meaning *Looking for meaning in religious language and imagery*
1	recognise words and items associated with religion, and recall the outline of stories	use their sense to explore and question religious stories, pictures and artefacts
2	describe some religious practices and events, and identify basic beliefs	suggest and begin the identify meanings behind religious imagery (story, symbol, picture, building...)
3	make connections between key events/stories in the foundation of a religious tradition and some beliefs/practices which developed from them	identify and describe some appropriate meanings for religious stories and imagery
4	describe and distinguish some key beliefs and practices of Christianity and two other religious traditions	explore and explain meanings conveyed to believers by religious stories, symbols and practices
5	identify religious questions and issues, and compare/contrast some key beliefs, explaining how these impact on personal, social and religious practice	understand and show how religious ideas and beliefs can be expressed thorough imagery and symbol, and use terminology appropriately
6	give a coherent account of the beliefs and practices of different religious traditions, and explain what it means to be committed to particular values and groups	understand and give examples of the range of imagery and terminology used in religion and account for different uses in specific faith groups
7	compare and contrast the principal beliefs of faith communities and their bearing on a range of human concerns	apply knowledge, skill and critical imagination in interpreting religious language
8	explain the relevance of religious beliefs and practices in their historical, social and cultural contexts, and understand some contemporary challenges to faith	offer valid interpretations of religious language in a variety of forms and contexts
9	evaluate the place of religious belief and practice in society and culture	make deductions about the function and importance of religious language

Figure 19: Steps approach – Staffordshire Agreed Syllabus

Learning from Religion

Issues *Exploring and understanding spiritual, moral and social issues*	**Lifestance** *Developing personal stances on related issues*
express their knowledge and experience of the world around them and of how people relate to each other	respond appropriately (eg with curiosity, sensitivity, imagination, thought) to things which they find interesting or puzzling
show some awareness of people's values and recognise some experiences that cause people to wonder and to question	express their own ideas of what is of value or concern to them
recognise attitudes and values that people have, and express ideas about right and wrong	relate their own values and concerns to the experience of others
describe situations where certain values are in evidence and understand the need to make moral choices	show respect for people's beliefs and values, and begin to be aware of their own questions and choices
make clear connections between personal standpoints and the actions people take	show awareness of some consequences of the particular beliefs and values they hold, reviewing them in the light of others' experiences and insights
describe different ways in which people respond to difficult or inspiring situations	give an account of their personal viewpoints on a range of issues whilst taking account of the views of others
give reasons for different responses to challenging issues in life	express an informed and reflective personal viewpoint, identifying influences on their own values and beliefs
carefully analyse creative responses which human beings make to life's questions	offer reasoned judgements on matters of belief and behaviour, based on open enquiry and the weighing of evidence
evaluate responses to moral issues and ultimate questions	present evidence for a personal viewpoint while offering objective arguments for alternative perspectives

KS 1
KS 2
KS 3
KS 4 & 5

The language of learning objectives

Learning about religion

- Know that, identify, name, describe, give an account of
- Understand that, how, why
- Explain the meaning of (why), importance of
- Be aware of
- Interpret

Learning from religion

- To develop own responses to
- Reflect on, the reasons for, the value of, the belief that, the role of, the idea that, the importance of
- Question

Figure 20: The language of learning objectives

Standards in RE

Most readers will be aware that QCA have published various documents relating to standards of achievement in the National Curriculum; for example the Exemplification of Standards booklets. More recently QCA has published an Exemplification of Standards booklet for RE.[2] This booklet is based on the 1994 Model Syllabuses and therefore, while helpful in many ways, lacks the distinctiveness of similar documents produced by a few local authorities.[3] It is, however, worth obtaining a copy of the QCA booklet if you are concerned about how to judge standards of pupils' written work. Of course such judgements are made easier if the planning is clear and the objectives are clear. In this section of the chapter we shall look at a particular piece of written work relating to the above topic 'Why are we here?'

Assessing a piece of written work

We cannot assess everything, and it is a good idea when planning medium-term to identify a particular task or activity that we will use for the purposes of assessment. If we look at the 'Why are we here?' unit we can see that planned into it is a summative assessment that involves the writing of a poem. An example from one Year 6 boy, David, is given below. Before we look at this and before we attempt to make a judgement it is necessary for us to understand the context in which this poem was written.

Context
This Year 6 group had been following the topic 'Why are we here?' They had been introduced to the nature of ultimate questions, partly through the formative assessment worksheet illustrated below, and had been provided with opportunities to reflect on issues arising out of the Genesis story of creation and the children's story *Dinosaurs and all that Rubbish*.(see Chapter 6 pages 90-91). The aim of this lesson was for the pupils to reflect on the beginning of creation and to express their thoughts and feelings about its value in the form of a poem. The specific objectives that the teacher set for this were:
• To think about how the world began
• To reflect on their own and others' responsibility for the Earth

---

Formative Assessment   **Why are we here?**

Questions, questions, questions?

In this topic we are going to explore different kinds of questions that people ask about life and the world around them

1 Look at this list of questions

a What was the date of the Battle of Hastings?
b Where are the Pennine Hills?
c Does God exist?
d What is a Mosque?

e Should we be kind to animals?
f Why did the world begin?
g At what temperature does water boil?

You may have come across questions like these in some of your lessons. Try and match these questions to subjects at school by putting the appropriate letter by the side of the subject.

History _____   RE _____

Science _____   Geography _____

2 Now consider the questions

What is a Mosque? _____   Does God exist?_____

Can you write down what is different about these two questions?

_____

_____

_____

_____

Figure 21: An example of formative assessment related to Year 6 Unit of Work

In this context David wrote the following:

> Flashing Stars
> Volcanoes erupting
> Poisoness air
> Lava pouring out
> Burning gasses
> Making our world
> Silence ....
> Things starting to grow
> Little things starting to grow
> Life beginning in a beautiful world
> Dinasours coming
> First birds whistling
>
> People came
> Some like to be here –
> Some spoil our precious world

How do we judge this poem in the light of the objectives for the lesson and the overall aims of this topic? We must ask ourselves, is it any good? How do we know?

Judging using RE-specific criteria

If there is a criticism to be made about teachers' comments about pupils' achievements in RE, it is that such comments often fail to refer to any specific RE criteria. I have shown this poem to many colleagues and most are agreed that this is a good poem. It is well written, despite the couple of spelling mistakes. It has a good form to it, language is well used and David makes good use of his imagination. However, if we were to rely solely on such judgements it would look as if we were judging a piece of English. How then can we make our comments specific to RE? The answer lies in referring to the two objectives, above, and to the mid-term unit plan. If we look at the three objectives in the first column we can see that it is the intention that pupils are able to

- Express their own beliefs and values about creation
- Express a judgement about the relationship between humans and the natural world
- Explain the meaning of creation stories.

As David is obviously making his own judgement about the need for humans to exercise stewardship towards the Earth, we can safely say that he is achieving these objectives. He is also successfully exercising a number of the skills, and the attitude listed in the fifth column. How then should we comment on his work?

Comment on David's work
In the light of what we have said in the previous section an appropriate comment might be:

David can draw meaning from the creation stories and other stories told as part of this topic. He shows sensitivity to the world around him and displays an ability to reflect deeply on important questions about the relationship between human beings and the natural world. He is able to make good use of his imagination to express his feelings about this.

As we mentioned when discussing levels in RE, above, it is often necessary to have more than one piece of evidence before making firm judgements about at what level pupils are working. Nevertheless, from the evidence of this poem we can say that David is achieving well in terms of the end of key stage descriptions for Year 6 pupils.

How much evidence?
This is a question that teachers often ask me on INSET courses. The first thing to be said is 'Avoid an over-burdensome and essentially meaningless "tick box" approach to assessment'. For this particular topic the teacher would have a written piece of formative assessment which will provide some initial information on how well pupils understand the type of questions that arise in RE lessons, and a written piece of summative assessment in the form of the poem. Certainly in David's case this would be enough.

However, there might be occasions when we want to consider more evidence. In the case of the other example unit of work, 'Loving and Giving', Louise wrote the following.

The Good Samaritan

One day there was a man on a donkey and then he got bullied
by some robbers and then a priest came along and took no notice
and then another man came by and took no notice. Then a another
man came along and he was a Samaritan and he bandged him
and then he put him on his donkey
and then took him to his home and
put him in his bed and geve him
a drink and apple and then they
lived happily ever after.

This piece of writing is evidence that Louise can, with a few local embellishments, retell the story of the Good Samaritan. It is probably reasonable to say as well that the writing provides some implicit evidence that Louise does understand the meaning of the story and so would be achieving the target of meaning highlighted in the left hand column of the unit. But we can't be sure, not least because the activity itself does not necessarily give pupils the scope to write about the meaning. In Louise's case we might look for other evidence, and this was forthcoming in a discussion about the story. During the discussion the teacher asked the class, 'Why do you think the other men didn't help the man?' One boy, Andrew, replied, 'Because they didn't want to get beaten up and robbed.' This may well be an accurate reading of the priest's and levite's motives but Louise's answer, 'They didn't think of the man. They only thought of themselves', displays quite a profound grasp of the meaning of the story and the issues within the broader theme of loving. With this additional evidence we may now want to say that Louise is achieving well.

Recording achievement in RE

There are various ways to record achievement in RE but the essential thing to remember is that recording should not become cumbersome and overly bureaucratic. It is generally agreed that the most useful methods of recording are:

- *Records of teacher observations.* This might be a record book with a page for each child on which you can record significant contributions made by a pupil in discussion. Pupils very rarely display great insight to order; rather comments made in unexpected or unrehearsed situations can be significant and display understanding and progress.
- *Portfolios.* It has become common practice for teachers to keep a limited number of pieces of work by pupils together with a suitable comment. So, for example, a portfolio on David would include his poem and the teacher's comment as written above. There is no hard and fast rule about this. Some teachers might like to keep a record of responses to specific assessment tasks, others may keep a more random selection.
- *Individual pupil profiles.* Many teachers use a record sheet that can be carried forward by a pupil throughout the school, or even the whole of his or her schooling. The best examples of these are simple and provide a clear focus of achievement against appropriate indicators such as attainment targets, programmes of study and pupil attitudes to work.

- *Pupil self-assessments.* It is important to involve pupils in their work and attainment. There are a variety of appropriate forms available for this which usually involve pupils in recording the objectives for topics , to record their own views on their strengths and weaknesses as well as how much they did or didn't enjoy the topic.[4]

Reporting RE

Good reporting depends on good recording because it is a distillation of what has been recorded. If recording is poor or vague then so will be the reporting. Unfortunately the kind of reporting we often see for RE is like the example below:

> Jill has worked hard this year. She has taken a real interest in her work, has completed her homework on time and has achieved above average results in her assessment.

The problem with such a comment is that while parents would be pleased to hear of Jill's hard work, it tells the reader absolutely nothing about her aptitude for RE. This report could be about any subject.

A good RE report should contain specific references to pupils' achievements against the syllabus' programme of study and attainment expectations. In short it is a good rule of thumb to remember that appropriate reporting should indicate

- What the pupils have been doing in RE
- How they are progressing
- Their grades or levels (perhaps with older children)

Conclusion

It is worth summarising the main points made about assessment in this chapter.

- Assessment is integral to learning and therefore should be built in to the planning of RE mid-term units of work.
- Assessment should be based on clear and achievable learning objectives.
- These objectives should be shared with pupils as much as possible.
- Assessment tasks should form part of the range of learning activities.
- There should be opportunities for pupils to respond at different levels.
- Assessment should provide reliable data for reporting on pupil progress and for curriculum development and improvement.

[1] QCA, *Non-Statutory Guidance on RE*, Qualifications and Curriculum Authority, 2000, pages 4-12

[2] QCA, *Exemplification of Standards in Religious Education*, Qualifications and Curriculum Authority, 1998

[3] See for example, Hertfordshire County Council, *Consistency in Teacher Assessment Exemplification of Standards*, 1996, and Hereford and Worcester County Council, *Consistency in Teacher Assessment Exemplification of Standards*, 1996

[4] See for example, Rudge, John, *Assessing, Recording and Reporting RE (A Handbook for Teachers)*, Westhill RE Centre, 1991 and Langtree, Graham, *Are You Ready? Developing quality religious education in the primary school*, RMEP, 1997

5 The teacher's role

Most teachers, when asked, will say that they entered the profession because of a sense of vocation. As one trainee said, reported in the *Guardian* recently, 'You carry yourself differently (as a teacher). I wanted to be able to say to myself, "I like you". I couldn't do that in my old job.'[1] So the motivation to teach is a deeply human thing. A reason why many teachers get so worried during Ofsted inspections is because they see their job as reflecting something of themselves. In teaching therefore there is a very personal dimension to being a good professional. This is certainly true of the RE teacher, where personal commitments and ideals are often part and parcel of the material being taught. This chapter looks at three elements of the RE teacher's role. First, there is the complex but highly important issue of the commitment of the RE teacher; second, some practical advice is given regarding dealing with controversial issues and pupils' questions in the classroom; third, we look at the less personal side of the job in terms of professional knowledge and abilities.

Commitment and the RE teacher

The development of a multi-faith approach to RE based on open enquiry brings the question of the teacher's role and commitment into sharp focus. The issues that surround this area can be encapsulated by the question 'What types of commitment can be expected of the RE teacher?'

In the past, when RE was indistinguishable from Christian nurture, this question did not arise. It was clear to everyone that the teacher's role was characterised by convergence. This means that there was no possibility of conflict between what the teacher believed, the content that was to be taught and the desired outcomes of pupils' learning. All these factors converged to assist the teacher in the 'passing on' of the Christian faith.

The emergence of the multi-faith approach to RE breaks the link between faith, content and aims. This is because, as John Hull has pointed out, such a view of religious education does not seek to promote convergence but instead requires divergence.[2] Divergence means that the personal faith of the teacher, the content, and the aim of what is being taught are no longer linked. For example, divergent teaching may involve a Christian teacher in the endeavour of teaching Judaism, not to 'pass on the faith' but to help pupils to gain knowledge of and insight into a religion which may not be their own. This requires a different approach from the teacher and demands a different set of commitments.

There was a time in the recent past when the answer to this question of teacher commitment was seen to lie in the neutrality of the teacher. But what does that mean? A number of writers[3] have pointed out that if neutrality means that teachers have no commitment whatever, this is not only a dangerous notion but also an impossible one. It is impossible because no human being is capable of being neutral in this way; it is dangerous because the teacher may not be aware of how she is in fact influencing the pupils.

Just to reinforce the point, let us take an example from my own experience. A friend of mine, an RE co-ordinator, was preparing to have her meeting with the Ofsted inspector on the Monday evening of her school's recent inspection. The inspector introduced himself as an atheist and announced that he believed the best RE teachers were atheists because they weren't biased in favour of any religion. What was so objectionable about this assertion was not the fact that he was an atheist, but the implication that the best teachers of RE are those who are not involved. It was as though he was saying that the best RE teachers are those who can keep a dignified distance from the content of the subject. Of course, this inspector hadn't had the opportunity to read this book!

Contrary to the inspector's view, it is the contention of this book that to be effective teachers of RE we need to engage in the same process as the pupils. This is the process outlined in Chapter 3, and the point being made here is that we too, as teachers, need to increase our understanding of the place of religion in people's lives by relating what we learn about the religions to our own deepest questions of meaning and purpose. And we need to care about this process as well. Nevertheless, does the fact that teacher neutrality is a dangerous, if not an impossible, notion mean then that RE teachers have to be believers?

In the conventional sense of being a Christian or Jew, this cannot, and many would say should not, be expected of a teacher of RE. This is because RE does not seek to promote a particular religion. However, as we have seen, what RE does seek to promote is an involvement in the process of what Fowler calls faith. We are seeking to enable our pupils to explore the 'big' questions of life, to see them as a challenge, to learn about religious perspectives on life and see them as a challenge to pre-conceived ideas of what is important in life, and so on. We are seeking to develop their 'individual patterns of belief', to enable them to become more sensitive and mature about religion and life issues.

Of course we all know that this is the difficult part. It *is* easier to present information about religions, even though we all aspire to going beyond that. But if we want our pupils to engage with the process, do we not have to engage with it ourselves? How many music teachers don't play an instrument? How many PE teachers don't play a sport? Now this does not mean that a RE teacher has to be a believer in the conventional sense. We don't need to engage ourselves *in* religious belief and practice. However, I think that what we have discussed so far does mean that we need to engage, ourselves, *with* religious belief and practice. One way of doing this as a teacher is to take part in courses that include visits to places of worship. The intention is to enable teachers to engage with people of the different religious traditions. It's rather more than just a religious tour. The results of such visits can be quite dramatic, as some of the evaluation comments below illustrate.

Evaluations of inter-faith study courses for teachers

'The whole experience of observing worship and talking to people in the faith communities brought the textbook images to life. It was an enlightening experience.'

'Memorable: I learned more about different faiths than by reading books.'

'This weekend has revitalised and inspired me.'

'It has deepened my understanding of faith.'

'A great spiritual and educational experience.'

'The Sunday was less beneficial to my school but very valuable for my own development.'

Figure 22: Evaluations of inter-faith study courses

So what we are saying here is that the best teachers of RE see such learning opportunities as part of their personal as well as professional development.

If we want our pupils to engage with the process of RE, then we need more than a passing interest in it ourselves if we want to enthuse them.

Dealing with controversial issues, including pupils' questions

The questions surrounding the commitment of the teacher easily spill over into matters concerning the classroom. How, for example should we answer pupils' questions such as 'Do you believe this, Miss?' The key is to think about the language that we use. The way we use language in RE lessons is crucial if we are going to communicate effectively and if we are to avoid accusations of 'pushing our ideas down children's throats'. In order to be clear about this, RE teachers have increasingly referred to 'owning' and 'grounding' language in the classroom.[4] Central to understanding these two terms is to understand the distinction between what we might call 'factual' statements and 'belief' statements. For example, a statement about where Jesus was born and when and where he lived is potentially open to historical research; whereas a statement like 'Jesus is the Christ who died to save the world from sin' is not. The latter is a statement of Christian belief.

We deal with both kinds of statement in the classroom and they can form part of pupils' questioning. For example, when following a topic on Easter a pupil might ask a teacher whether he believes that Jesus rose from the dead. This is a difficult question and one that refers to an aspect of belief. What if the teacher is not a Christian? How might he respond? If he uses owning and grounding terminology then he should be able to own his belief. That is not to say that he should be careless with his language so that he answers, 'No, I think it is a conjuring trick with bones!' He might be better to use words like 'Well I'm not a Christian and so I find it hard to believe,' or a Muslim teacher might reply, 'As a Muslim I don't believe that but we Muslims do believe that Jesus was a very important prophet of Allah.' Nevertheless, whatever the owning reply might be, the teacher has a duty to ground the pupil's question with the addition of, 'But of course the resurrection is very, very important for all Christians. It is probably the most important event in the life of Jesus.'

Such open use of language should enable all participants to be themselves in RE lessons and so give the subject some integrity. It is also an honest approach and an educative one. It is important that pupils grow to understand that on some matters people differ in their beliefs.

Professional knowledge and abilities

Developments in RE since 1988 have placed increasing demands upon primary teachers' subject knowledge. As well as mastering the content of the National Curriculum subjects, it is expected that a modern day primary teacher should know enough about world religions to teach the programme of study in the local agreed syllabus. In practice this usually means knowledge of Christianity and at least two other religions. Moreover, a specialist primary RE trainee must have a detailed knowledge of the QCA Model Syllabuses. This is a tall order for anyone, especially when it is realised that knowledge of religions is only part of an effective RE teacher's subject knowledge.

Mere knowledge about religions can result in a limited form of RE teaching that concentrates on a transmission model of education that is concerned with imparting information. As we have seen in Chapters 2 and 3, it is important that an RE teacher also understands something about the nature of religion in a generic sense, and then applies this understanding to the nature of RE as a curriculum subject. In short, it means understanding how the knowledge of and about religion and religions contributes towards the process of teaching and learning in RE. This means, in very practical terms, enabling pupils to learn *from* religion as well as learning *about* religion. A variety of teaching resources and approaches, as outlined in Chapters 6–8 is helpful here but two crucial aspects of enabling pupils to learn from religion is firstly to plan for it, and secondly to employ effective questioning in the classroom.

Short term (lesson) planning

Effective lesson planning depends on there being in place an effective and progressive Scheme of Work based on the principles outlined in the previous two chapters. The Scheme of Work is the responsibility of the RE co-ordinator. A scheme that includes good mid-term planning should enable all those in school who teach RE to identify appropriate aims, objectives and teaching methods for a particular lesson. An effective lesson plan should contain:

- A statement of aim(s) for the lesson based on the Scheme of Work
- Learning objectives identified under the headings of knowledge, understanding and reflection
- A sequence of teaching and learning activities, indicating how the class is to be arranged and organised
- A statement about evidence of learning taking place
- Resources to be used
- Any differentiated activities
- The lesson's contribution to assessment of the pupils

The example overleaf is a lesson based on the mid-term plan 'Why are we here?' on pages 50-51 of Chapter 4.

Lesson title	Class	Pupil no	Length
How did the world begin?	6	25	75 mins

Aims and link with previous lessons

- Pupils will have been introduced to the question 'Why are we here?' and had the opportunity to reflect on issues arising out of the Genesis story and the children's book *Dinosaurs and all that Rubbish*
- This lesson's aim is for pupils to reflect on the beginnings of creation and to express their thoughts and feelings about its value

Objectives	Sequence of activities	Class organisation
		Individual and paired
AT1 to know • that for religious people stories can make sense of puzzling questions **AT1 to understand** • how stories can express values and meaning **AT 2 to think about (reflect upon)** • how the world began • their own and others' responsibility for the earth	• Teacher recaps on previous lesson: short discussion of stories and issues • Pupils brainstorm the word 'creation' • Pair work: discuss own ideas about how the world began, pupils to write down own ideas • Teacher lead plenary in response to task • Teacher explanation of next task: pupils to write own poems using 'brainstormed' words and pupils' own ideas and beliefs • Plenary: pupils read out poems	
Evidence of learning		
Quality of discussion Quality of poems	Resources	
Assessment	Stories, paper, worksheets or books on creation stories for extension activities	
Poems that express a sense of mystery and express a judgement	Differentiated work; extension activity(s) Research creation stories from different traditions	

Figure 23: Lesson plan: 'Why are we here?'

The key to achieving the aims for the subject in this particular topic and lesson is the quality and clarity of the objectives. As we have already mentioned, effective RE teaching needs a balance between knowledge, understanding and reflecting on or thinking about what has been learnt. Clear, achievable and assessable objectives in each of these three areas are vital for good pupil achievement in RE. It might be useful to re-read the section on objectives in the previous chapter.

Asking the right questions

A teacher who encourages pupils to ask questions and who handles such questions effectively ensures, in the long run, a suitable learning environment for RE. Such an environment will enable pupils to feel confident to discuss sensitive and, sometimes, personal issues. This can be further facilitated if the teacher is skilful at asking open-ended questions that are designed to stimulate enquiry in the pupils.

There are many different types of questions that can facilitate learning in RE. A selection to help you is given in the box below.

Types of effective questions

Questions can be asked for different purposes. Below is a selection of types of questions and their purpose in the process of teaching and learning in RE.

'Where is Jerusalem?' to recall information

'Why do Muslims go on hajj to Makkah?' to develop understanding

'Is the Buddhist monk praying or meditating?' to apply knowledge and understanding to new situations

'What did your visit to the Gurdwara tell you about how Sikhs understand service to others?' to encourage analysis

'How do you think Jesus felt just before he was crucified?' to encourage an exploration of ideas and feelings with no set answer

'What is your opinion about...?' to encourage evaluative thinking

'How has our study of Sikhs been useful for our understanding of equality between people?' to encourage application of knowledge

---

Figure 24: Types of effective questions

Checklist

It might be helpful as a way of summarising some of what we have said above in the form of a checklist against which you can measure your practice.

A checklist of questions for primary RE teachers

1 Ethos
- Do I encourage pupils to ask questions and listen attentively and respectfully to others?

2 Subject knowledge
- How good is my knowledge of the content of RE appropriate to my school's Scheme of Work and the pupils who I teach?
- How good is my understanding of the process of teaching and learning in RE?

3 Planning
- Are my objectives clear and appropriate and do I share them with my pupils?
- Do I plan using knowledge, understanding and reflecting objectives?
- Do I plan a variety of teaching methods appropriate to the lesson?
- Do I plan for a variety of effective questions depending on what it is I want pupils to learn?
- Do I plan for a variety of resources?

4 Classroom practice
- Are my lessons well paced?
- Do I use a variety of organisational strategies such as whole class, individualised, pair work, group work etc.?
- Do I employ a variety of teaching and learning methods such as pictures, video, stories, artefacts, visits etc.?
- Do I encourage the use of specialist vocabulary and technical terms in my teaching?

Figure 25: A checklist of questions

The RE-co-ordinator

Many readers of this book will either be, or aspire to be, the school's RE co-ordinator. This in modern parlance means being a subject leader in RE. This short section will indicate some of the roles and duties of an effective RE co-ordinator. If you wish to consider the role of subject leader in RE in more depth then you should obtain a copy of *Effective Subject Leadership in Religious Education* published by the Association of RE Inspectors, Advisers and Consultants (AREIAC).[5] This is a detailed publication that follows the Teacher Training Agency's criteria for subject leadership. For our purposes here it will be useful to provide a general checklist of the duties of the RE co-ordinator, over and above those already mentioned for all teachers of RE (above).

These duties can be classified under different headings.

Professional subject knowledge
As well as the aspects of subject knowledge described above for all teachers of RE, a co-ordinator needs to
- know what the legal requirements for RE are and understand the issues surrounding the place of RE in the curriculum
- update herself regularly, keeping in touch with local and national developments in RE. A good way of doing this is to become a member of the Professional Council for RE (PCfRE). Details from CEM, Royal Buildings, Victoria Street, Derby, DE1 1GW, Tel: 01332 296655

The RE Curriculum
The co-ordinator is responsible for the following aspects of the curriculum;
- Making sure that senior management understands the time requirement for RE (5% curriculum time) and the funding implications for adequate resources that will help promote effective teaching. Also, with senior management, writing and keeping up to date a yearly development plan for the subject
- Creating and writing (ideally collaboratively) a policy for RE. For guidance on this try *How to Write your School Policy for RE* by Geoff Teece, Westhill Publications 1994. Available from Westhill RE Centre, University of Birmingham, Westhill, Selly Oak, Birmingham B29 6LL. Tel: 0121 415 2258
- Producing a clear and progressive Scheme of Work, which includes long and mid-term plans, with advice on differentiation. The first part of this book should help you with this as will *How to Write your Scheme of Work for RE* by Geoff Teece (1996), available as above.

- Providing clear guidance on assessment arrangements, recording and reporting RE (see Chapter 4 of this book).
- Obtaining and managing a varied collection of resources for RE. How these are stored, for example, can determine how well they are used. Far too often schools have good RE resources but few teachers use them. So, for example, if you have collections of artefacts make sure there are notes with them so that the non-specialist can use them!
- Monitoring the effectiveness of the RE curriculum. With the co-operation of colleagues, regular monitoring of the effectiveness of the Scheme of Work, the adequacy of resources etc.

Providing guidance for colleagues
A really effective RE co-ordinator is not only a highly competent teacher of RE but is also able to develop good relationships with colleagues. One of the great services a co-ordinator can do for the subject is to demystify it, make it attractive and exciting and be able to give colleagues the confidence to teach it well. One effective way of doing this is to make sure attractive displays of RE work are always prominent in school. Having established good relationships a co-ordinator can be a guide for her colleagues in the following ways:

- Be aware of the fears, confusions and concerns of colleagues about RE
- Advise and help colleagues identify and write clear objectives for RE, to think about assessment and help them adopt a variety of teaching methods and use a variety of resources
- Support colleagues in their teaching through lead lessons and/or team teaching and share each others' examples of good practice and good work produced by pupils
- Lead staff meetings on RE, provide school-based INSET, act as the liaison person between different phases of schooling, or across a cluster or within a pyramid
- Establish contacts with outside agencies, especially local religious communities, and encourage colleagues to use visits as part of their RE programme.

[1] The Guardian 9.4.99 p19
[2] Hull, John, 'Open Minds and Empty Hearts? Convergent and Divergent Teaching of Religion' in *Studies in Religion and Education*, Falmer Press 1984
[3] See for example Hulmes, E *Commitment and Neutrality in RE*, Chapman 1979
[4] For a fuller explanation of this see, Read Garth, et al *How do I Teach RE?* Westhill RE Centre, 1998, pages 67-68
[5] Grove, Julie & Teece, Geoff (eds), *Effective Subject Leadership in Religious Education*, AREIAC 1999

6 Using Stories

In recent years there has been some attention paid to the contribution that story in RE can make to such initiatives as the literacy hour. While this is understandable, it should be emphasised that story has a distinct contribution to make to RE teaching in its own right.

Why tell stories in RE?

There is an old Jewish saying, 'God created man because he loved telling stories'. This certainly points to the truth that for human beings, story has played a central role in enabling them to make sense of themselves and their world.

In tribal societies, stories were told, and still are told, from one generation to the next.

All civilisations have their stock of stories that have preserved continuity in beliefs, values and attitudes. All the great religious teachers have used story as a powerful educational device. Religion has always been clothed in the poetic language of story and myth.

The stained glass windows in local churches point to the importance and value of story in communicating essential truths. In more recent times, we find that the most popular television programmes in India and amongst many Indian people in this country are the serialisations of the great Hindu epics such as The Mahabarata. These great tales of the gods and heroes of the Hindu religion are awaited as eagerly as many western couch potatoes await the next episode of *Neighbours* or *Eastenders*.

Today we find the emphasis in education on the acquisition of skills and knowledge as information. We seem so concerned with the physical and the measurable that anything that eludes this is looked upon with a certain amount of scepticism.

However, since the passing of the 1988 Education Reform Act, emphasis has been placed on the importance of the spiritual dimensions of the curriculum. At a conference held at Westhill College in January 1993, HMCI Stewart Sutherland, referred to this spiritual dimension as being concerned with 'human flourishing'. This recognises that education must enable pupils not only to calculate, measure and live life in purely materialistic terms, but to seek other dimensions of human consciousness and endeavour; in short, to be able to formulate beliefs about the ultimate meaning, purpose and significance of life in general and of their lives in particular.

Therefore whilst the knowledge of facts and information about religion is important, RE has a particularly important contribution to make to the spiritual, moral and social development of children.

This means that teachers of RE are not simply concerned with what we may call the top layer of the mind, the layer that is able to retain information and reproduce it for the purpose of passing examinations. It is a layer that has little effect on deciding who we are and how we behave towards others. If RE is to contribute towards the development of pupils' spirituality then it must touch deeper levels of the human mind and psyche. These are the levels which effect our emotions and have a more lasting effect on our development as persons.

Story is the ideal vehicle for reaching the parts that mere information cannot touch. Stories do have a surface meaning but it is from a deeper level of meaning that pupils can discover personal meanings for themselves. For stories at a deep level can speak to each one of us individually, to the circumstances of our lives in the here and now. One cannot plan or legislate for these personal meanings but the way in which a child responds personally to a story can have a profound and lasting effect on how they see themselves, those around them and the world in general. Stories, in short, have the power to affect the deepest levels of our consciousness.

Stories have many other characteristics which make them an essential element in good RE teaching.

- Stories structure the world. Just as a story has a form and a purpose, stories can tell us that life on earth is not chaotic and meaningless but has a pattern and can be full of meaning.
- Stories can expand the imagination, introducing us to people and worlds beyond our immediate experience. In a very real sense they can enable us to enter into dialogue with other people, hence enabling us to develop important skills essential to RE, such as sympathy and empathy.
- Stories provoke insight into ourselves. They provide a way of understanding our hopes, fears and desires.
- Stories provide opportunities to explore the mystery and beauty of the world. They can encourage us to think more deeply about our responsibilities towards the natural order and can help us to come to terms with the darker side of natural forces.
- Stories can help us to deal with disturbing and upsetting episodes in our lives by providing a distancing device. Stories for children about the death of a pet or a grandparent can help them come to terms with such events.

- Stories can help us to become aware of the nature of story itself (an explicit concern for Key Stage 2 pupils). They can introduce children to the nature of poetic language, to simile and metaphor and the different story forms (such as myths, legends, allegory and biography).
- Stories can be a very accessible way of understanding a religious tradition. The Good Samaritan helps children explore questions about loving behaviour but it also helps them understand something about Christianity, particularly the concept of love as charity.
- Stories can help us to explore fundamental moral questions. They have the power to introduce children, through their characters, to the human capacity for good and evil.

What kinds of stories are suitable for RE?

Stories come in many shapes and forms and, especially with today's developments in technology, are not merely confined to book form; there are television soap operas and stories told through pictures only. It is important to remember that stories began as a telling, so it is the quality of story that is important rather than the form it comes in.

We might be able to get clearer about what stories are most suitable for RE if we take a TV soap opera as an example. Some may want to say that the soap opera has little in it of value for RE; that it is 'ephemeral ... and merely reflects, and thereby reinforces social mores. Its primary function is to entertain and it rarely does more than that'. But is this always the case? The answer would seem to be, very often. However, it need not be. Roy Hattersley, writing in the *Sunday Times* (7th March 1993) bewails the deterioration in his most beloved soap opera, *Coronation Street*. His main criticism is that the Street's 'characters were once a convincing commentary on the way we live now'. But, 'any resemblance to you and me is now purely coincidental.'[1]

What he is saying here is very important in helping us answer the question we started with. For *Coronation Street* to be valuable it does not have to be a documentary, it does not have to be true in the sense that it deals with actual people. It can caricature, but these caricatures have to speak to us as humans in our human condition. Once we stop believing that, the characters lose their power to move us, to force us to ask questions about ourselves. The raison d'etre of the programme becomes merely that of diversion, of entertainment, to fill a gap in our highly pressured lives.

Therefore, an important criterion for a story to be valuable for RE is that it must have depth. It should hold up a mirror to life and pose questions to us. Humankind has a wealth of these stories: myths, allegories, fables, parables and legends are some examples. Myths are perhaps the type of story with most depth. It is unfortunate that the word 'myth' has come to be seen as synonymous with 'untruth'. These stories which have endured for millennia bear witness to the fact that humans can go beyond the immediate conditions of their existence. They bear witness to the power of human imagining and they 'answer', not in the sense of scientific proof but rather poetic truth, some of the most fundamental questions of human existence. In one sense, it is possible to say that these stories attempt to answer the fundamental question 'What does it mean to be human?' Arising out of this question are other questions which great stories seek to provide answers for. These are questions to do with our origins, the purpose, value and meaning of our lives, authority, our identify and our destiny. We have already considered the importance of these kinds of questions in Chapter 3. However, as a reminder, we are thinking about a type of question such as 'How should we treat other people?' 'How should humans treat the world and other creatures?' 'What is happiness?' 'What does it mean to belong?' 'Are people more important than things?' Stories which deal with such diverse questions have great potential for use in RE.

In summary then there are three main areas from which we can draw stories for primary RE. First, there is the great stock of myths, legends and fables which have been characteristic of all civilisations. Second, there are the stories from the sacred scriptures and traditions of the major religions of the world, and third, there is the wealth of contemporary children's literature in both picture book and novel form. These areas are not mutually exclusive but they can act as a guide when selecting.

Choosing the 'right' stories

The first criterion for successful story telling is to choose a good story. The story should display some of the characteristics that we have discussed in this and the previous section. It is well worth considering what do not count as appropriate 'stories' for our purpose.

- A story is not a report. Newspaper editors may refer to what appears in their papers as 'stories'. However, these 'stories' have a limited capacity to capture attention and are unlikely to be told again and again, at least not in the form they appear in the newspaper.
- A story is not just a succession of events.
- A story is not a series of descriptions, no matter how descriptive or colourful.

The kind of stories we have been talking about are first and foremost, narratives about people, and in some cases animals, birds etc. They involve people in events, the progress of which arouses interest from the start. The interest is sustained through various steps mounting to a climax when curiosity is satisfied.

The Bible

It seems that ever since Ronald Goldman published his research into children's religious thinking in 1964 and declared that the Bible is not a children's book, primary teachers have been unsure as to what to do about Bible stories. In some cases, it has been believed that young children in school should not be told them because they cannot understand them. In other cases, they have formed the sole resource for teaching RE, but teachers have told them because they believe they should be told without really being able to say why.

We do our children no service at all if we deny them this rich source. Not telling children Bible stories not only denies them a heritage but a profound source of insight into their experience. Whilst it is prudent to have criteria for selection of Bible stories, we should look beyond mere intellectual understanding as the only criterion. Like all great stories, Bible stories are powerful vehicles of communication. They operate at different levels of meaning and significance and we can return to them time and time again, finding in them richer and deeper levels of meaning. This is because the Bible is essentially a book about human experience.

It is often said that the Bible is more like a library than a single book. Within the Bible we can find an enormous variety of literature. There is the history of a people, there is legend, parable, allegory, poetry and myth.

The Bible, like all sacred scripture, helps humans to expand their understanding of truth. Western society still, unfortunately, labours under the misunderstanding that truth can only be found in the scientific disciplines; that all else is mere personal opinion or belief. The Bible can help us and our children counter this erroneous belief. There are at least four categories of truth into which the Bible can provide insights:

Firstly, through its myths and parables the Bible points us to the life of experience. It makes sense in and of our experiences by pointing more deeply into what it means to be human.

Secondly, because it is the story of a community; the story of the Israelites, the Bible tells us that what community values most. It is possible to say that the values of the Bible are true in as much as they stand up in the experience of that community.

Thirdly, the Bible points us to dimensions beyond the everyday experience of coping with the mundane aspect of our lives: 'the groceries of what is'. Characters in the Bible are often recorded as having overwhelming experiences that, no matter how fanciful or miraculous, make sense to them in relation to other aspects of their lives.

Finally, because the Bible also contains historical narrative, it can help children understand something of the time and place in which the events of the Bible occurred.

What is important, however, is that the Bible is most effective in RE when stories are chosen which enable the pupils to engage in the process as outlined in Chapter 3.

The example below shows how this can be done.

Story/selected passage	Key Stage 1 Content focus (topic)	Key stage 2 Content focus (topic)
The Creation Genesis Chapter 1	The world around us • Foster awe and wonder • Awareness of beauty and mystery • Celebration and joy of the Earth Questions to raise • What is precious? • What things are beautiful about the world? • What is valuable? • Should we be thankful for the Earth? • Who made the world?	How did the world begin? Was the world made for us? Creation stories Questions to raise • How did the world begin? • Was the world made for us? • What are Creation stories? • Can Genesis be true?

Figure 26: An example of using a Bible story in Key Stages 1 and 2

Stories from other traditions

All the major religions of the world provide a rich source of stories for primary RE. This section is designed to help you by describing the nature and character of some of the important stories within each of the major traditions. The resource list has selected examples of the stories described here.

Will using stories from such diverse sources confuse the children? I would suggest not. As we have noted, all good stories have a depth that allows us to reflect on, broaden and deepen our understanding of the issues and questions which affect our lives as humans. And the best stories can be told because they have the potential to speak to the deeper levels of our minds. The great religious stories do not, as we saw when discussing the Bible, need to be fully explained or used for moralising. This can destroy the essential nature of these stories and inhibit their power to enliven the imagination. With children in their early years it does not matter if they know or understand that a particular story is a Buddhist story; they will not be able to conceptualise Buddhism anyway unless, of course, they have been brought up within a Buddhist tradition. Rather, if the story is a good one and illustrates a point or theme that has been discussed with the children, then it will work.

Of course the stories from the traditions reflect the nature and characteristics of those traditions, as well as communicating the beliefs and values that followers seek to express in their lives. Therefore pupils at the upper end of Key Stage 2 can begin, through story, to understand the essentials of Buddhism, Sikhism, Islam, Hinduism and Judaism. The same can be said, of course, for Christianity.

Buddhist stories
There is a great tradition of story telling within Buddhism. Like Jesus, Buddha often communicated the great truths of existence by means of story. Moreover, the power of these stories is that they are left to make their own point. It is up to the listener to find the meaning within each story and apply it to his or her own experience. It is often said that an essential quality of Buddhist stories is that of mind consciousness. They bring the listener face to face with an important truth about life and leave him or her to reflect on it. For example, the story of Kisagotami (sometimes called the Mustard Seed or Poppy Seeds) is a story told without sentimentality of the inevitability of death.

Different Buddhist groups have a variety of key stories which reflect the central characteristics of their tradition. Therevada Buddhists use the story of Gautama Buddha to reflect qualities in Buddhist life such as world renunciation, self-reliance and the virtues of love and compassion. These qualities reflect what lies at the heart of Therevada monastic life (*sangha*). Thus the story of Gautama Buddha is an appropriate means by which pupils can understand some of the values of Buddhism and the practices of the Therevada lifestyle.

Mahayana groups use stories of the Bodhisattvas (Buddha-to-be: those who have put off their liberation, *nirvana*, in order to help others to escape from suffering). The most famous is Avolokiteshvara, whose great compassion is manifest in contempory figures such as the Dalai Lama.

Perhaps the richest source of story from the Buddhist tradition for use in Primary RE are the 500 or so Jataka Tales. The word *Jataka* means 'birth story' and each of these stories recalls an incident in one of the previous lives of Buddha. Tradition says Buddha told these stories to his followers to illustrate the Buddhist moral perfections such as generosity, patience, wisdom, renunciation, compassion and virtuous conduct. However, it is believed that many of these stories came from a rich stock of Indian folklore. Because in many of his past lives Buddha was born into the animal kingdom, many of the stories are animal stories, albeit focusing on an animal or bird of unusual wisdom! There are similarities here for westerners with the fables of Aesop.

A selection of Jataka Tales is included in the resource list.

Sikh stories
Stories told within the Sikh tradition, which can provide a resource for RE, originate in the life and teaching of Guru Nanak. At the age of 30 Guru Nanak had a mystical experience of God and this led him to become an itinerant teacher, accompanied by Mardana who provided musical accompaniment to Nanak's 'songs', which were revelations of his divine message and later comprised part of the Sikh holy book *The Guru Granth Sahib*.

Nanak's teachings arose out of his experiences of God and the theological disputes he engaged in on his travels with the religious leaders of his time. The earliest collection of these stories are the *Janam Sakhies*, or life evidences. These stories are not biographies of Nanak because they do not tell of historical events in the life of the Guru. The writers of the stories used the events of Nanak's life to communicate the essential teachings of the quality of all human beings, the virtues of honesty and hard work, and the important Sikh concept of *Sewa*, the idea that you can only love and serve God if you serve humanity. Selected examples of Sikh stories can be found in the resource lists.

Hindu stories
To the uninitiated the Hindu tradition might seem like an unfathomable and complicated tradition from which to identify appropriate stories. For a start there are so many scriptures!

To make matters easier it is important to understand that Hindu scriptures can be classified under two headings. Firstly there are the scriptures called *shruti* (revealed truths). These scriptures are believed to have been revealed to holy men who interpret them for those who seek spiritual guidance. They are ancient and contain the scriptures referred to as the Vedas and the Upanishads. The second group of scriptures are called *smriti* (remembered truths) and these form what is usually referred to as the popular religious literature of the tradition. The *smriti* contain the great Hindu epics such as The Ramayana and The Mahabharata and the later scriptures called The Puranas. The stories contained in these scriptures address the religious beliefs, ideals and values of the Hindu way of life. The most famous section of the Mahabharata is the *Bhagavad Gita*. The 'Gita' is a conversation between Arjuna, who is preparing to fight a battle, and his charioteer who is in fact Lord Krishna. The message of the 'Gita' is that devotion to God (*bhakti yoga*) is the highest form of worship and this explains its great popularity amongst many Hindus. The Ramayana, which contains the story of Rama and Sita, contains the universal message that good triumphs over evil. Many teachers will be familiar with this story as it is recited during the festival of Diwali. Finally the Puranas tell the stories of the 'gods'. The most popular, the *Bhagavad Purana*, tells of Vishnu and his avataras, including Krishna. The Puranas also tell of the other main Hindu gods, Shiva and Brahma.

Versions of these stories can be found in Indian bookshops; one of the most accessible books is called *Cradle Tales of Hinduism*.

Muslim stories

Islam has a wonderful tradition of literature and suitable stories for primary pupils are easily available. Stories derived from the Qur'an and the Hadith (traditions of the prophet) can help pupils understand the teachings of Islam as well as appreciate the universal values such as love and kindness to all people and the animal kingdom. There are also books available that tell the stories of the prophets of Islam and the Caliphs (those leaders who came immediately after the prophet).

Many of these stories are available from The Islamic Foundation and although written for Muslim children they can easily be used for all pupils in RE lessons.

Jewish stories

Judaism contains a great wealth of stories derived from its sacred literature, its legends (*aggadot*) and folk tales (*maaysiot*). The Jewish fairy tale is a genre unto itself and forms a rich source of story. The great universal theme of good and evil can be explored through such stories which can also teach us something about the Jewish view of life in which God can defeat the evil impulse (*Yetzer ha-ra*). An excellent collection of

Jewish fairy tales can be found in *Elijah's Violin* by Howard Schwartz. Of course the Tenakh (Jewish Bible) contains many rich stories associated with the sacred year of the Jews, a good example being the book of Esther.

Preparing a story

We all admire great story tellers at work. They capture our attention and keep us spellbound. Whilst we may not class ourselves as experts in this field, there are ways of making story telling more effective.

The following points are worth bearing in mind:

- Only choose to tell a story you like. If you do not like a story, do not tell it. You cannot possibly do it justice, and your own negative feelings may be passed on to the pupils.
- You have to know your story. Try not to tell a story that you have not already read yourself several times. Try to get 'inside' the story, and become familiar with its characters and plot and the story's conclusion.
- You can read the story or tell it from memory. If you are reading the story, know it well enough to not have to keep concentrating on the text. If you decide to tell it, make an outline of the story, either in your head or on paper. This will help the vitality of the story not to be lost.
- Practise reading or telling the story out loud to yourself before reading or telling it to your pupils.
- Use your imagination when practising the story by focusing your mind on the particular group of pupils that you intend telling the story to. This will help in making it appropriate to the age and aptitude of your group.

Preparing the pupils

If the story is to have an effect we have to make sure that the pupils are adequately prepared. The first requisite is, obviously, to make sure the pupils are sitting comfortably and in a position to see and hear you easily.

Some story tellers like to use an 'entering' device by which children can understand that they have entered the world of story. Some suggestions for these entering devices are given in *A Gift to the Child: Teachers' Resource Book* (see resource list for details). These can include a story hoop. The hoop is covered in colourful materials such as crêpe paper and the children and teacher hold onto the hoop; the idea being that all are joined together and focused on the space in the middle, out of which the story will come. Other entering devices are a lighted candle, sitting on the story rug, or closing the eyes when a bell is sounded to signal the start of the story. It may be that our sole aim in telling a particular story is to create an atmosphere and simply tell the story and leave it to make its impact.

However we may feel, sometimes, that for a story to have maximum effect, an activity or activities need to be introduced beforehand. We can refer to these as focusing activities. The following examples may be used to suit a particular situation.

Listening tasks

Here we can allocate to the pupils, either individually or in groups, a variety of listening tasks. Each individual or group has the task of listening for aspects of the story such as what is said or done by various characters, important words said by characters, and so on.

Direction setting

This may be necessary, particularly with early years children. The teacher can use a carefully framed question to focus the pupils' attention or may feel the need to introduce some unfamiliar vocabulary. For example, in preparing to tell a Biblical story like The Good Samaritan, it may be wise to have prepared some flash cards with the words, Jesus, Samaritan, priest, temple. A preliminary discussion of these words can help the pupils understand the point of the story more clearly and set the story in its context. Other direction-setting examples can include the period of history, part of the world or religious tradition in which the story is set.

Raising an issue

A story may be chosen and told for the purpose of raising an issue relevant to a particular theme which the teacher wishes to introduce. A story can also help throw light on an issue already raised in class.

Telling a story

When reading or telling the story, the best advice is usually to allow it to do its own work, by resisting the temptation to interrupt to ensure that listeners 'get the point'. An exception might be made in the case of children in the early years, where the attention-span is limited. They are likely to be most involved when the reader or teller makes frequent eye contact, while pauses to examine the illustrations or to clarify their feelings and reactions can help to hold their interest to the end. For older pupils, the choice between telling or reading will depend upon a variety of factors, including pupils' ability and readiness to give their attention, the claim and power of the written word to convey the exact point of the story, the poetic appeal of some passages, and (when using picture books) the need to focus on and support the illustration.

Following up a story

You are probably familiar with a number of activities for developing or following up a story. The story may be told in its own right but often it is told within the context of a theme, issue or other ongoing classroom activities. The possibilities for following up stories are varied but a few suggestions below are offered as guidance.

Written responses
- a letter to or from one of the characters
- a newspaper report
- a poem

Drawing, painting or collage work

Drama
- an enactment of the story
- a contemporary version
- a mime

Alteration of the ending in writing or drama
- so that a different point is made
- so that an alternative solution is found

Extend the story in different directions
- invent new characters who can give their responses to what has happened in the story

Two examples: The Easter Story for Key Stage 1

The Easter Story is one that many teachers have hesitations about, mainly because of the supernatural elements. First, find a good, yet simple, version of the story like the one printed below. In this version the focus is on Palm Sunday, Good Friday, and Easter Day. Next, prepare some appropriate focusing activities and think carefully about the kind of questions you may use to stimulate discussion. Examples are included below, along with suggestions for follow up activities.

One day when Jesus was a grown-up man, he decided to visit the city of Jerusalem.

He told his friends that he wanted to ride a donkey into the city.

'Why does he want to ride on a donkey?' thought his friends.

They didn't argue with him. They did what he said and found a donkey.

Crowds of people gathered to see Jesus. They had heard a lot about him and they wanted to see him.

Some people said that he was a very good teacher. Others said that he could make sick people well. Others said that he was their new king. Some said that he was God's son.

There was a great deal of excitement as Jesus rode into the city.

Some people put their coats on the ground for the donkey to walk on. Others cut branches from the palm trees to spread in front of the donkey. Some remembered lines from one of their old poems:

> Look your king is coming to you!
>
> He is humble and rides on a donkey.

'Oh!' thought his friends. 'That's why Jesus wanted to ride on a donkey. Perhaps he is telling us that he is our king.' This made them shout and sing a lot louder.

There were some people who didn't like this at all.

They didn't like some of the things Jesus said. They didn't like some of the things Jesus did. They didn't like people saying that he was a king. They didn't like people saying that he was God's son. They became very angry.

Jesus is killed

Soon after his visit to the city of Jerusalem, Jesus went to a garden to pray.

One of his friends named Judas came to the garden with some soldiers.

Judas had betrayed Jesus to his enemies. He showed them where he was.

The soldiers took Jesus to the chief priest.

The chief priest asked Jesus, 'Are you God's son?' Jesus said, 'I am.'

'He says he is God's son. Nobody should say that. He is a liar, he must die,' said the chief priest.

Jesus was taken away. He was beaten with a whip. The soldiers dressed him up like a king and made fun of him.

Some people called out, 'Nail him to a cross and let him die.'

The soldiers put a crown made of sharp thorns on his head.

Then they took Jesus to a hill near the city.

There they nailed Jesus to a cross made of wood.

One of Jesus' best friends, John, was standing near to the cross. Jesus' mother, Mary, was there too.

Jesus said, 'John, look after my mother. Mother, take care of John.'

Jesus then looked at his enemies. He spoke to God and said, 'Father, forgive them. They don't understand what they are doing.'

Then Jesus bowed his head and died.

Strange and mysterious happenings

Jesus' friends took his body down from the cross. They put it in a cave and rolled a big stone in front of the entrance. It was late on Friday afternoon.

On Sunday morning, some of Jesus' friends went to the cave. The large stone was rolled away.

Jesus wasn't there! An angel was there.

The angel said, 'Jesus is alive. Go and tell all his friends.'

Later that day, two men were walking to a town called Emmaus. They were friends of Jesus and were very sad. They had not heard that Jesus was alive.

A man joined them on the walk. He talked to them about Jesus.

When they arrived at Emmaus, the two men asked the stranger to come and eat with them.

During the meal the stranger said thank you to God for the food. This was just like the way Jesus used to do it. Then the men knew that this was Jesus.

Back in Jerusalem, the other friends of Jesus were sad and frightened. They were hiding in a little room. Suddenly Jesus was in the room with them. He told them not to be frightened. The he shared some food with them.

'It is Jesus!' they said. 'He is alive.'

Then Jesus disappeared from their sight.

Reproduced from Christians 1. *Westhill Project RE 5–16*

Focusing the story

- Ask the children what comes to mind when they think about Easter.
- Ask the children if they know why Christians celebrate Easter.
- Do they know anything about Jesus and what happened to Him?
- Have an artefact or object in the classroom for each part of the story and discuss its significance. For example, palm cross, hot cross buns, Easter egg, empty cross.
- Have a theme corner in the classroom for new life including, perhaps, seemingly dead twigs with buds on them.
- Tell the story in three stages over a period of days.
- Tell the children a story beforehand like *The Very Hungry Caterpillar*, to introduce them to the idea of transformation and new life.

Talking about the story

These are some examples of interpreting and applying questions that might help conversation.

- Why is such a sad story like the death of Jesus remembered on a day called 'Good Friday'?
- Why do you think people spread branches in front of Jesus?
- Can you think why Jesus rode on a donkey?
- Do you know what a mystery is?
- Why do you think Christians think this story is a mystery?
- Can something be all around us and not seen by us?
- Do you know anything that comes alive again after being dead?
- What do you think people mean when they say Jesus is alive today?

Such questions are not intended to elicit right or wrong answers. They are offered as means to open up discussion to give children something to think about.

Following up the story

- Display a chalice and patten with wine and bread, to help children reflect on the symbolic meaning of the resurrection
- Make an Easter garden
- Bake hot cross buns, decorate eggs, make Easter cards
- Visit a local church, and look for Easter symbols
- Listen to music inspired by the Easter story, eg *The Messiah*
- Look at pictures/videos showing Christians celebrating the Eucharist

Using a modern fable at Key Stage 2

Dinosaurs and All That Rubbish by Michael Foreman is a story about a greedy man who almost destroys the Earth until 'put right' by a dinosaur. The story opens up numerous questions about humankind's relationship with the natural world and provides opportunities for exploring religious beliefs concerned with this.

Dinosaurs and All That Rubbish

The story begins with the man who is not content, and bored with his life on Earth. He is fascinated by a star that he can see, far off, in the sky. He tries to reach it but can get nowhere near it. He decides that he must make his workforce build him a rocket.

The man owns many factories and the smoke, fumes and waste from them are making a terrible mess of the planet. The Earth is in such a mess that nowhere can be found to launch the rocket.

At last the rocket is launched and the man reaches his star. However, there is nothing to see or do on this star. All that can be seen is another star in the distance. The man decides to fly to that star (which he does not know is the Earth he has just left).

Meanwhile, back on Earth the rubbish and heat disturbs the sleep of the dinosaurs. The Earth cracks and the dinosaurs come back to life. When they see what human beings have done to the planet they are disgusted and quickly get to work to make the place habitable again.

Meanwhile, the man returns to Earth thinking he has found a new paradise. He decides to stay, claiming it for himself. But the dinosaurs do not let him have it all his own way. They succeed in making him understand that the Earth is for everyone and should be valued.

Focusing activities

- Show pupils a picture of the Earth, preferably taken from Space. Use a bank of questions to help children respond. For example:
  - What do you see in this picture?
  - Is Earth the only planet?
  - What is our planet made of?
  - Do you think that our planet has always been here?
  - How do you think it began?
  - Will our planet ever disappear?
  - What kinds of things do people need to live on our planet?
  - What do plants and animals need to live on our planet?

– What do you enjoy most about living on planet Earth?
– In what ways could our planet be made a better living place for people?

• Make a display of natural objects such as sand, rocks, wood, plants and pictures of animals.

Talking about the story

Here are some questions intended to enable you to develop a conversation about the story.

– Why do you think the man wanted to fly away?
– What do you think about how the man treated the Earth?
– How should we treat the Earth?
– Why is it precious?
– Who does it belong to?
– Should we share the Earth with animals?

Following up the story

• Read with the children other stories on the same theme; for example, *The Glass Cupboard* by Terry Jones.
• Read the creation story from Genesis and explore the meaning of the story in terms of the Christian concept of stewardship.
• Read a Hindu creation story and discuss the implications of the belief that all beings are part of God.
• Look at pictures/videos of religious groups at worship and discuss with the pupils the ideas that some people feel the need to thank God for the Earth.
• It is also interesting to tell this story during Harvest Festival time, if you hold one in school.

[1] These quotations were taken from the Roy Hattersley article printed in *The Sunday Times*, 7 March 1993

A selection of sources

General
Barratt, M (1994), *Bridges to Religion* (BR) (The Warwick RE Project) Heinemann

Ganeri, A (1994), *Out of the Ark: Stories from the World's Religions*, Simon and Schuster

Grimmitt, M et al (1992), *A Gift to the Child*,(GC) Simon and Schuster

Jackson, J (1994), *Share Our World*, Simon and Schuster

Newby, M, *Thinking about Actions, Attitudes and Values in the Classroom: a guide to the use of story in spiritual aspects of education*, British Humanist Association, 47 Theobalds Road, London WC1X 8SP

Palmer, S, Breuilly, E (1992), *A Tapestry of Tales*, Collins

Buddhism
There are several sources for Jataka Tales. Dharma Publishing of California do a series of well illustrated picture books. Windhorse Publications do a series of excellent stories. These and the Dharma books are available in most large centres belonging to the Friends of the Western Buddhist Order. The best place to contact is Windhorse Publications, 11 Park Road, Birmingham B13 8AB.

Clear Vision Trust also do an excellent video package called *The Monkey King and Other Tales*. Available from The Clear Vision Trust, 16/20 Turner Street, Manchester M4 10Z

Broadbent, L & Logan, J	2001	*Under the Bodhi Tree*	RMEP

Christianity

Barratt, M	1994	*An egg for Babcha* (BR)	Heinemann
Barratt, M	1994	*Lucy's Sunday* (BR)	Heinemann
Bennett, O	1986	*Colin's Baptism*	Heinemann
Broadbent, L & Logan, J	2001	*A Very Special Sunday*	RMEP
Cole, O & Lowndes, J	1995	*The Birth of Jesus*	Heinemann
Cole, O & Lowndes, J	1995	*The Story of Easter*	Heinemann
Cole, O & Lowndes, J	1995	*Stories Jesus Told*	Heinemann

Cooling, M	1996	*Story and Drama Toolkit*	Bible Society
Cooling, M	1996	*Writing and Poetry Toolkit*	Bible Society
Fidge, L	1994	*Bible Activities* (Age 5-7)	Folens
Grimmitt, M *et al*	1992	*Aideen's Book* (GC)	Simon & Schuster
Grimmitt, M *et al*	1992	*A Story of Hallelujah* (GC)	Simon & Schuster
Grimmitt, M *et al*	1992	*Natalie's Book* (GC)	Simon & Schuster
Grimmitt, M *et al*	1992	*The story of Bernadette* (GC)	Simon & Schuster
Palmer, J	1995	*Easter* (5-11)	Stanley Thornes
Self, D	1986	*Stories from the Christian World*	Macdonald

Hinduism

Cole, O & Lowndes, J	1995	*The Birth of Krishna*	Heinemann
Cole, O & Lowndes, J	1995	*The Story of Prahlad*	Heinemann
Gavin, J	1986	*Stories from the Hindu World*	Macdonald
Grimmitt, M *et al*	1992	*Kedar's Book* (GC)	Simon & Schuster
Grimmitt, M *et al*	1992	*A Story of Ganesh* (GC)	Simon & Schuster
Jaffrey, M	1985	*Seasons of Splendour*	Pavilion
Mitchell, P	1989	*Dance of Shiva*	Hamish Hamilton

Islam

Aggarwal, M	1984	*I am a Muslim*	Franklin Watts
Barratt, M	1994	*Something to Share*	Heinemann
Broadbent, L & Logan, J	2001	*Watching for the Moon*	RMEP
Grimmitt, M *et al*	1992	*The story of Bilal* (GC)	Simon & Schuster

Grimmitt, M *et al*	1992	*The story of God's words to Mohammad* (GC)	Simon & Schuster
Grimmitt, M *et al*	1992	*Yaseen's Book* (GC)	Simon & Schuster
Khattab, H	1987	*Stories from the Muslim World*	Macdonald
Maqsooq, R	1995	*A story of Id*	Heinemann
Stone, S	1988	*Eid ul Fitr*	A & C Black

Books published by Muslim sources
(Muslim Educational Trust = MET, Islamic Foundation = IF)

Hendricks, M	1991	*Muslim Poems for Children*	IF
Kayani, M S	1981	*Assalamu Alaikum*	IF
Kayani, M S	1981	*A Great Friend of Children*	IF
Kayani, M S	1982	*Love All Creatures*	IF
Murad, K	1982	*Love Your Brother Love Your Neighbour*	IF
Murad, K	1982	*Love Your God*	IF
Murad, K	1983	*Love at Home*	IF
Sarwar, G	1981	*Islam for Younger People*	MET

Judaism

Barratt, M	1994	*The Seventh day is Sabbath*	Heinemann
Broadbent, L & Logan, J	2001	*Let My People Go*	RMEP
Cole, O & Lowndes, J	1995	*The Jews leave Egypt*	Heinemann
Cole, O & Lowndes, J	1995	*Moses on the Mountain*	Heinemann
Grimmitt, M *et al*	1992	*Rebecca's Book* (GC)	Simon & Schuster
Grimmitt, M *et al*	1992	*A Story of Jonah* (GC)	Simon & Schuster

Hannigan, L	1985	*Sam's Passover*	A & C Black
Lawton, C		*Matza and Bitter Herbs*	Hamish Hamilton
Patterson, J	1987	*A Happy New Year*	Hamish Hamilton
Schwartz, H	1983	*Elijah's Violin*	Oxford

Sikhism

Arora R		*Guru Nanak and the Sikh Gurus*	Wayland
Bennett, O	1984	*Kikar's Drum*	Hamish Hamilton
Cole, O & Lowndes, J	1995	*Guru Nanak*	Heinemann
Grimmitt, M et al	1992	*Sabjit's Book* (GC)	Simon & Schuster
Grimmitt, M et al	1992	*The Story of Nanak's Song* (GC)	Simon & Schuster
Solomon, J	1980	*Bobbi's New Year (Baisakhi)*	Hamish Hamilton

Also available in some Indian shops

| Singh, M | 1990 | *Guru Nanak* | Hemkunt Press |
| Singh Bros | 1996 | *Bed Time Stories* | Amritsar |

7 Visiting places of worship

Visiting places of worship is a vitally important part of any RE programme. Not only does it bring the subject to life but it provides a vital opportunity for personal experience. The beauty, atmosphere and sacredness of many places of worship are impossible to create in the classroom. Pupils are able to meet and talk with practising members of religious communities and are able to learn from experience, which will prove to be a deeper form of learning than merely being told about it or experiencing it through video.

There are some basic principles to keep in mind when planning to visit. First, try to involve the children as much as possible. Perhaps they could write a class letter requesting a visit to follow up your initial contact. Try to visit a building when it is in use. This, of course, is not always possible, especially visits to churches which may only hold services on Sundays. Whatever, the situation regarding this, try to make sure you establish a clear contact with a person who can talk to the children. Let them know exactly what you want to achieve from the visit. It is very easy for a visit to lack focus and so become just 'a look round'. Also you should keep in mind the aims and purposes of RE so that visits don't merely concentrate on things like architecture, for example. There are many reasons for visiting a place of worship. The table below is intended to help you focus the purpose of your visit as clearly as possible.

You can visit a place of worship to

- Experience its atmosphere and its worship
- Meet and talk to its members as well as key figures such as the Imam or the priest
- Explore its architecture and elements of the building
- Identify and name important parts of the building
- Investigate meanings of worship and symbolism
- Extend knowledge and understanding of a religious tradition in terms of its key beliefs and values
- Examine in detail a particular aspect, sect or expression of a tradition
- Reflect on personal responses to the experience
- Raise questions about the building or/and the tradition

Figure 27: Reasons for visiting places of worship

When planning your visit make sure you find out answers to some of the following questions.

Are there any special dress requirements?
Are there any points of etiquette to bear in mind?
Will you be offered any food, and if so what and why?
Are photographs allowed?

Is it appropriate to make a donation? It is usually good practice to take with you, or send with thank you letters from the children, a small financial donation to contribute towards the community's funds. However, some Gurdwaras, for example, will not accept money in this way. This is because by welcoming you they are performing *sewa*, selfless service without any expectation of reward. If this is the case, all Gurdwaras have a collection box in front of the Guru Granth Sahib and you can give each child a coin to put in the box when they visit the prayer hall. Alternatively you can donate some fresh food or milk just like members of the community will do. This also applies to visits to Hindu temples.

Advice on visiting places of worship

Visiting a Christian place of worship

Of course there are many different types of Christian place of worship. You could choose an ornate building like an Orthodox Church or a sparse Quaker meeting house. It is good to vary visits in order to explore different forms of Christian worship. If you visit a fairly conventional church, make sure you concentrate on the aspects that relate to worship rather than treating it like a church study, which you might be doing as part of history. Things to point out are the altar, lectern, pulpit etc. Some of the symbolism in churches may well help with exploring the variety of Christian worship. If at all possible try and go to a church during a service. There are weekday services in some churches. For variety, it may be worth considering visits to an Orthodox church for liturgy or a Black Pentecostal church for praise.

Advice on etiquette
There are no special requirements in most churches except respectful behaviour.

Visiting a Gurdwara

Sikh worship has a number of interesting elements that could be explored. A visit to the Gurdwara could include experiencing the *Akhand* path (the continuous reading of the Guru Granth Sahib) and the receiving of *Kara*

Prashad (a sweetmeat offered in the prayer hall). There would also be the opportunity to experience *langar* (a shared meal given to all as an example of Sikh *sewa* (service to others) and the Sikh stress on equality of all humans). A visit to experience Sikh congregational worship, probably most likely on a Sunday, which includes the singing of *shabads* (hymns from the Guru Granth Sahib), would be good.

Advice on etiquette

Everyone will be required to cover their heads and remove their shoes. Whenever you enter the prayer hall, a small bow in front of the Guru Granth Sahib may be expected. It is a way of expressing respect and showing politeness to the community. Always avoid turning your back on the holy book or pointing your feet towards it. When in the prayer hall, you will be offered *Kara Prashad*, which is a sweet substance. It may not be to everyone's taste. If you want some, take it in both hands. If not, no one will be offended. In a Gurdwara, never take food if you do not want it. It is seen as wasteful. It would be unusual for you not to be offered langar. With a group of children, this is likely to be a coke and a biscuit, or something similar.

Visiting a Hindu temple

The best time to visit is when *aarti* is being performed. In most Hindu Temples in this country this will mean between 10.00 and 11.00 in the morning. There is, usually, an evening aarti. The new Hindu Temple in Neasden, North London, has more than two aartis per day but the most popular for visits is late morning. It is important to prepare the children for this visit. The inside of a temple is bright with many images, *murtis*, of the gods. It would be helpful to explain to the children that Hindus don't actually worship lots of gods but for them Brahman, ultimate reality, is the world's soul and all the images are really expressions or aspects of the one reality. Perhaps explain how one person can be many things, a mother, a wife, daughter etc. In British Hindu temples the main images are usually aspects of Vishnu, particularly Krishna/Radha and Rama/Sita and Shiva.

Advice on etiquette

You will need to remove your shoes before entering the temple. There are no special requirements regarding dress and no head covering is needed. Before leaving, you will normally be offered a gift of fruit or sweets. It is polite to accept. Hindu temples are good places to take photographs, but always ask permission.

Visiting a mosque

The best time to go is on Friday lunchtime for *juma* (congregational) prayer. In big mosques there may be as many as 2000 people there for this prayer. Get there early enough to hear the *adhan* (call to prayer). On a Friday there will also be a sermon (*khutbah*), and very often this is in English as well as Urdu. You will see Muslims offering their own *du'a* prayers, as well as the formal set *salah* prayer. Mosques tend to be symmetrical, which illustrates the central Muslim belief in *tawhid* (the oneness and unity of God). You can point out the *mihrab* (the recess in the wall that faces Makkah and the minbar (a small 'pulpit' from where the imam delivers the khutbah. If you can't go on a Friday, check the local prayer timetable for other *jamaat* prayers (this means the daily prayers in the mosque).

Advice on etiquette

Everyone will be expected to remove their shoes and all girls should dress modestly (trousers are best) and cover their heads. Boys are not required to cover their heads but it is often polite to do so, as many Muslim men wear caps during prayer. Do not point the feet towards the *qibla* wall (that facing Makkah). Male and female may be asked to sit separately but often you would sit together as a group at the back of the prayer hall.

Visiting a synagogue

As this is likely to be a weekday, avoid Fridays, as Jews will be getting ready to celebrate *shabbat*. Also avoid festival times (check with the Shap Calendar available from the National Society RE Centre, tel: 0171 932 1190). As there will be no worship taking place, a good guide will be able to show you the *ark* (cupboard) where the torah scrolls are kept, as well as the *bimah* (platform from where the torah scrolls are read). Look out also for the *ner tamid* (the eternal light burning above the ark). They will also be able to show you the *tallit* (prayer shawl) worn by men. If you can strike up a good relationship with a Jewish community, an evening visit during festival times can be rewarding.

Advice on etiquette

All males are required to cover their heads, and in orthodox synagogues men and women sit separately during worship.

Visiting a Buddhist centre

Many Buddhist 'places of worship' are small, often houses, although there are some larger buildings. The best thing to ask your guide to concentrate on is describing the shrine with its Buddha image, flowers, candle, incense and seven bowels to welcome the guest. Remember that Buddhists don't worship Buddha but use the image to be reminded of the qualities of Buddha. The main practice in Buddhist centres is meditation, and it would be good to ask about this and perhaps practise some. Be sensitive about this and make sure everyone at school, and parents, know what you are doing. If you do get the chance to do some basic meditation, it will be concentration on the breath. If you want to explore this further, it is worth getting hold of a video published by Clearvision Trust, tel: 0161 839 9579, *Buddhism for Key Stage 2*). You can use such a video and this advice in the classroom if you cannot or do not want to make a visit.

Advice on etiquette

You will be expected to remove your shoes. Some Buddhist monks are not allowed to touch women, so do not expect to shake hands. There are no dress requirements but there may be quite a long time sitting on the floor.

A focusing activity for follow up work

You may wish to engage your pupils in a variety of activities after a visit, including discussion, written work, thank you letters, paintings etc. It is always a good idea before asking the children to do these things to enable them to reflect and re-imagine the visit to focus their attention.

One very helpful way with older primary is to ask them to write a cinquain. It is possible to do this together, as a class, with younger pupils.

Firstly, write a list of adjectives describing what they experienced on the visit.

Secondly, a list of verbs.

Thirdly, some nouns.

Fourthly, a four-word statement that sums up the visit.

Then arrange the lists in the following order:

– One word title

– 2 adjectives

– 3 verbs

– 4 word statement

– 1 noun.

An example of a cinquain:

Worship
Surprising, challenging
Waiting, watching, listening
Faith displayed and observed
Commitment

8 Using visual resources

We cannot always study religion at first hand. Fortunately the use of artefacts, pictures, videos, and now ICT have become established and vitally important means of teaching RE.

Artefacts

Using artefacts in RE is now an established method of teaching. Artefacts help make the subject 'real' for the pupils. They enable the teacher to bring something of a tradition into the classroom. They enable pupils to explore at first hand some of the rich religious meanings that they contain. In fact artefacts offer learning opportunities for pupils which cannot be achieved by other resources or methods. Nevertheless many teachers need help and guidance in the appropriate use of artefacts. The term 'appropriate use' refers to both the importance of handling artefacts sensitively and with respect, as well as how to make use of them in a way that is educationally worthwhile.

Using artefacts

Artefacts can be used in the classroom in a variety of ways. It is possible to group types of use under two headings, of passive use and active use. Artefacts can be used passively in the sense that displays of artefacts can create an atmosphere and an environment in which pupils can acquire a sense of a religious tradition. Such displays can foster positive attitudes of respect and interest. In terms of active use, artefacts can be used as a stimulus for discussion, for story writing, for drama work and art work (for example making other artefacts). Artefacts are also good for enabling pupils to investigate a religion. One useful method developed at Westhill RE Centre by Kathy Wedell uses an approach where groups of pupils are given two artefacts, for example two Muslim prayer mats or two Hindu *murtis* (or deities). Such pairs of artefacts can also be 'cross-religious', for example a Roman Catholic rosary and a Muslim *subha* (prayer beads). The pupils are then given a series of instructions to work through. These instructions are:

- Make a list of the similarities and differences between the two objects.
- List a number of questions you have about the objects.
  - The teacher then gives the pupils some information in the form of a workcard or textbook in order that they can find answers to the questions raised. What usually happens is that a greater knowledge

provokes a fresh set of questions and so the next instruction is:
- Look at the cards (textbook) and see how many of your questions you can answer.
- List any further questions that you now have about the artefacts

The beauty of this is that it gives the pupils a context in which to explore the artefacts. If pupils are just given a single artefact it is much more difficult to work with. Usually they would have to rely on their own experience, which may be very limited. Whilst this approach may be more suited to older and brighter primary pupils, an excellent approach to using artefacts with younger children can be found in *A Gift to the Child* (see book list in Chapter 6).

Sensitivity to artefacts

A teacher needs to be aware of the possible sensitivities associated with any artefact. Artefacts are not manufactured for educational use like photo packs or textbooks. They have their existence within a religious tradition and religious community and therefore it is possible to offend. For example don't leave a Qur'an open on a Qur'an stand as part of a display, be careful how you handle the Qur'an and keep it wrapped in a high position. Be careful with the Sikh kirpan. Many Sikhs would not draw the kirpan out of its sheath because it is an object for defence rather than offence. It is not possible to go into detail here about every sensitivity and tradition but you might like to consult any of the books recommended at the end of this chapter.

Pupils need to handle artefacts if they are to be truly useful in RE. This requires that the teacher set a good example in the way that artefacts are handled. Pupils can receive messages about the teacher's attitude towards a particular religion by the way she handles an artefact.

Establishing an artefact collection

Many schools now like to develop their own collection of artefacts. Some share the cost in a cluster. Whatever the case, some advice on what a basic collection might contain would be useful.

Buddhist artefacts
Statues or pictures of Buddha
Shrine set
Stupa
Mala (necklace, 108 beads used in devotional practice)
Wheel of Life poster

Prayer Wheel
Offering Bowls
Danaru (a small drum used in worship)
Images of different Bodhisattvas

Christian artefacts
Bible
Prayer Book
Crucifix
Cross
Palm Leaf cross
Baptismal candle
Paschal candle
Advent candle
Chalice
Paten and wafers
Icons
Rosary
Prayer ring
Greeting cards: Baptism, Confirmation, Marriage, Christmas, Easter,
    First Communion
Salvation Army flag

Hindu artefacts
Religious Posters or plastic statues of Hindu Gods and Goddesses,
    e.g. Hanuman, Ganesh, Laxmi, Durga Shiva, Krishna, Vishnu,
    Rama-Sita, Shiva-Parvati
Aum symbol
Doll in Indian dress
Puja tray
Divas
Garlands
Incense sticks

Islamic artefacts
Qur'an
Qur'an stand
Prayer carpet
Prayer beads
Headcap
Compass
Posters

Plaques
Greeting cards (Eid)
Miswak
Halal toothpaste
Halal soap
Examples of calligraphy, eg. the name of Allah the Shahadah

Jewish artefacts
Torah Scroll
Yad (pointer)
Tallith (prayer shawl)
Skull cap
Menorah and Hanukiah
Mezuzah
Seder plate
Hallah bread cover
Havdallah set
Shofar (Ram's Horn)
Kiddush Cup
Hagadah
Matza Cover
Gregor (used at Purim)
Dreidel (used at Hanukkah)
Cards (eg. Pesach, Hanukkah, Bat and Bar Mitzvah)

Sikh Artefacts
Guru Granth Sahib
Kanga (comb)
Kirpan (sword)
Kaccha (shorts)
Kara (bracelet)
Romalla (cover for scriptures)
Chauri (waved over Guru Granth Sahib)
Turban
Wedding bangles
IK Onkar symbol
Religious posters of the Gurus, Amritsar

Books about artefacts

Draycott, Pamela, *Religious Artefacts: Why? What? How?*, Christian
Education Movement

Gateshill, Paul and Thompson, Jan, *Religious Artefacts in the Classroom*, Hodder and Stoughton

Howard, Christine, *Investigating Artefacts in Religious Education: A Guide for Primary Teachers*, RMEP

Logan, John, *Artefacts for an Occasion*, BFSS National RE Centre

Wedell, Kathy, *Making the Most of Your Artefacts*, Westhill RE Centre

Using pictures for teaching

Most religions have aspects which can only be fully expressed visually.

One of the great advantages of using photographs in the teaching of RE is the possibility of bringing into the classroom what would otherwise be inaccessible aspects of the world. We cannot, unless we are very lucky, take our pupils to visit the Ka'bah in Makkah or experience the *Shabbat* meal in a Jewish home. Indeed for some of us it is difficult even to visit a Hindu temple in this country. What we can do, however, is to bring these visual aspects of religious belief and behaviour into the classroom in the form of content-rich, technically excellent and religiously authentic photographs.

Of course, photographs are not the same as the 'real thing'; they are a snapshot of time stood still. However, this sometimes has a distinct advantage over our usual impressionistic view of life gained from direct experience, which may be grasped only fleetingly. The photograph that 'freezes' a moment in time and space gives the observer time to examine certain features more closely. It can also allow a reflective approach to what is observed, something which may not always be possible during moments of direct experience.

In our RE lessons we need to encourage pupils to look closely at good quality photographs. At the same time it is essential that we as teachers are clear about what we want pupils to look for and what kind of responses we hope they will make.

Obviously an important reason for using photographs is to enable pupils to increase their knowledge and understanding of religious beliefs and practices by providing them with visuals that are rich in content.

However, using pictures in RE is not merely about gathering information about a religion. RE is essentially about the study of meaning. Therefore we should be asking our pupils both to encounter and to interpret the pictures. Interpreting requires us to move to a deeper level in our interaction with the pictures. The most immediate way to begin to interpret religious meanings is by engaging in face to face dialogue with people who have a religious faith. It is, after all, through human beings that religious meanings are mediated; that is why the encounter with religious believers is seen as such an important aspect of RE teaching.

Personal encounters with believers are not always possible or practical. Photographs can provide a good alternative, alongside video, books and artefacts. Good photographs for RE show members of religious traditions expressing religious meaning through their behaviour. They illustrate committed religious people expressing through their actions what they think is important about life. Pupils can be enabled to interpret meaning from such photographs by concentrating on the main theme or focus of the picture. Most will only be able to do that by being informed by the teacher of the religious meanings expressed in any particular photograph. It is helpful to pupils if teachers can explain to them the significance of the activity taking place in the photograph as well as explaining some of the beliefs and values being expressed. This will then enable the pupil gradually to develop 'layers of meaning' associated with that particular religious activity.

It is then important to help the pupils to apply the meanings encountered in the photograph to their own lives. This stage of the process is important for RE, for as we saw in Chapter 3 religious education is not just about gaining a knowledge and understanding of religion. It should involve pupils in applying what they have learnt to their own concerns about living. Therefore, in discovering the meanings expressed in the pictures, they may discover meaning in their own lives. By applying interpretations of the pictures to themselves, their understanding of their own feelings, commitments, beliefs and values is deepened and clarified.

Moreover, as we state constantly in this book, RE should also enable pupils to relate what they learn about religious belief and practice to the kinds of experiences we all share by virtue of our humanity. Good pictures have the potential to raise the fundamental or ultimate questions that human beings are constantly struggling with simply because they are human beings. So questions about origins and destiny, meaning and purpose, authority and identity are categories of questions that underpin much of our shared experience of life in terms of our relationships with one another, the lives we lead and the views we take of humanity's part in 'the scheme of things'.

What we have described here is an important part of the process of RE because it involves pupils in interpreting content and applying their interpretations to the wider world around them, to contexts outside their own immediate concerns. Therefore, while it is important for pupils to interpret religious meaning in terms of their own concerns (a process which we have called 'applying'), it is also important for them to take a step further and synthesise this by applying what they have learned to some of the fundamental issues and questions that concern the majority of human beings as they seek to construct meaning in their lives.

Thus, the process described in this section contains the following elements:

Encountering: What can I see here?
Pupils are introduced to the visual and helped to explore the content at a phenomenological level. They may return later to find deeper levels of meaning.

Interpreting: What is the main focus of this picture?
Pupils are encouraged to interpret the content of the picture in terms of the main focus or major themes in the picture.

Informing: What religious ideas/concepts are expressed in this picture?
The teacher introduces key ideas/concepts.

Applying: Does this picture arouse any feelings in me? Has the content of this picture anything to do with me?
Pupils interpret content and apply their interpretation to themselves and their understanding of the world, feelings, beliefs and values.

Synthesising: What issues or questions about life in general are raised for me by these questions?

Pupils interpret content and apply their interpretations to the wider world around them, to contexts outside their own immediate concerns.
It might be helpful to use the following questions with pupils:

• What are the people in the picture doing?
• Why are they doing it?
• How does the picture make you feel?
• What does the picture make you think about?
• Is there anything that you do that is like what is shown in the picture?

The elements of the process described here can be expressed in a diagram in circular rather than linear terms. This is to show the active and always continuing nature of discovering meaning in RE. For example, we do not just encounter the picture once and once only. Having gone through the process of applying and synthesising, pupils can return to the picture and possibly appreciate deeper levels of meaning, both in the picture, the particular tradition and life itself.

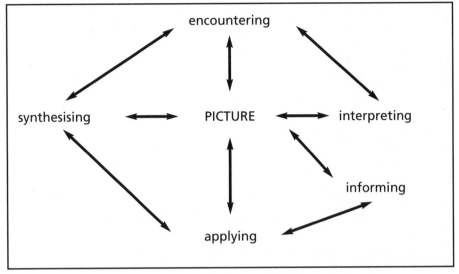

Figure 28: Exploring the process of RE through pictures

Useful sources for artefacts and pictures

The Westhill Project
Westhill RE Centre
Westhill College, Selly Oak
Birmingham B29 6LL
Tel: 0121 472 7248
Poster packs on all the major world faiths.

Pictorial Charts Educational Trust
PCET, 27 Kirchen Road
London W13 0UD
Tel: 0208 8567 9206
A wide variety of pictures, posters and wallcharts. Brochure available.

Philip Green Educational Limited
PGE, 112a Alcester Road
Studley
Warwickshire BV80 7NR
Tel: 01527 854711
Picture packs, slide-sets and filmstrips.

Folens Publishers
Albert House, Apex Business Centre
Boscombe Road
Dunstable LU5 4RL
Tel: 01582 472788
Photopacks & Posterpacks. Brochure available.

Christian Education Movement
Royal Buildings
Victoria Street
Derby DE3 1GW
Tel: 01332 296655
A comprehensive collection of booklets and posters. Brochure available.

The Islamic Cultural Centre and London Central Mosque
146 Park Road
London NW8 7RG
Tel: 020 7724 3363

Iskon Educational Services
Bhativedanta Manor
Letchmore Heath
Watford
Herts WD2A 8EP
Tel: 01923 857244
Hindu artefacts and other resources.

Gohil Emporium
381 Stratford Road
Sparkhill
Birmingham B11 4JZ
Tel: 0121 771 3048
Religious artefacts from India. Price lists available.

Degh Tegh-Fateh
117 Soho Road
Handsworth
Birmingham B21 9ST
Tel: 0121 515 1183
All kinds of Sikh religious artefacts, books and audiovisual resources.

Religion in Evidence
Unit 7
Monk Road
Alfreton
Derbyshire DE55 7RL
Tel: 01773 830255
Religious artefacts and posters.

RE and the internet

Trainee teachers will be very aware of the requirement to become competent in the use of ICT. Some CD Roms for RE are available but the best ICT resource for RE is the internet. With this in mind we have included below a short list of recommended websites which we believe are useful to the RE teacher.

General sites

www.re-xs.ucsm.ac.uk
RE-XS Religious Education Exchange Centre. This is a very good interactive site for both teachers and pupils. It has detailed coverage of the six major religions as well as new religious movements and non-religious worldviews.

www.theresite.org.uk
Provides very good links with other schools.

www.staplefordcentre.org
Has a good list of recommended sites.

www.culham.ac.uk
Provides excellent pictures, illustrations and text for Christianity. Good links.

www.sln.org.uk/re/
This is the Staffordshire LEA RE site. It is excellent and includes examples of stories from the major traditions that can be printed off. It also contains details of the Agreed Syllabus and the 'steps' approach to assessment (see Chapter 5).

Websites for information on the world religions

Buddhism
www.buddhanet.net
www.edepot.com/buddha.html
www.dharmanet.org
www.ciolek.com/WWWVL-Buddhism.html

Christianity
www.cofe.anglican.org
www.cafod.org.uk/schools.htm
www.canterbury-cathedral.org
www.internetdynamics.com/pub/vc/christianity.html

Hinduism
www.geocities.com/Athens/Styx/7153/Hinduism.html
www.hindunet.org/god/

Islam
www.islam101.com
www.islamicity.org
www.al-islam.com
www.al-islam.org

Judaism
www.aish.com/wallcam/
www.holidays.net/highholydays/
www.jewfaq.org
www.judaism.about.com/religion/judaism/mbody.htm

Sikhism
www.sikhs.org
www.sikhseek.com

Videos for RE

BBC TV

Pathways of Belief 7-11 years.
An excellent series covering aspects of Islam, Hinduism, Sikhism, Christianity and Judaism

Watch 5-7 years
Faith stories: key stories from Christianity, Judaism, Islam
Places for worship, Christianity, Judaism, Islam
Festivals and celebrations

Channel 4 TV

Quest 7-12 years
Animated World Faiths. An excellent series of ten programmes. The programme on Guru Nanak recently won a prestigious TV award.

Stop Look Listen
Water, Moon, Candle, Tree, Sword. A new multi-faith series for early years pupils.

For Buddhism try the excellent Clear Vision video packs *The Monkey King* (available from Clear Vision Trust 16/20 Turner Street, Manchester M4 10Z) and *Buddhism for Key Stage 2.*

9 Collective worship

The relationship between RE and collective worship

Some RE advisers discourage their teachers from thinking of RE and collective worship as two sides of the same coin. This is understandable. Firstly by discussing the two, confusion can arise about the distinctiveness of each. Secondly, it can add to the misunderstanding that an RE co-ordinator should be responsible for collective worship. Rather it is the headteacher who is ultimately responsible, though the RE teacher often has a part to play in giving advice to colleagues on collective worship. It is important that all involved are quite clear about the distinctions between the two areas.

The 1988 Education Act provides for both RE and collective worship. The inspectorate has usually recommended that there be 5% curriculum time devoted to RE. This is in addition to time spent on collective worship. This is reinforced in the DfE Circular 1/94. RE and collective worship are, therefore, separate activities, although in a primary school they often reinforce each other.

Another reason why RE Advisers are reluctant to mention collective worship in the same breath as RE is the fairly common perception that one activity (RE) is relatively non-controversial and the other (collective worship) is highly controversial. Maybe this is because, in the words of John Hull, people understand RE to be concerned with 'speaking about God' while collective worship is concerned with 'speaking to God'.[1] This suggests that that collective worship might be at odds with the educational philosophy of critical enquiry that forms the basis of most modern approaches to RE. The problem with this is that it is rather simplistic. Firstly it assumes that worship can't be educational and secondly it gives the impression that the approach to RE taken in this book, for example, is not controversial when quite clearly it is.

Circular 1/94

In recent years this concern over the educational validity of collective worship has been fuelled by the appearance of DFE *Circular 1/94: Religious Education and Collective Worship*.[2] This circular proved to be very unpopular within the profession and calls for its abolition are still being heard. It was the 1944 Education Act that made collective worship a compulsory part of the school day. The 1988 Act maintained this but sought to make the nature of collective worship more explicit. It states in Chapter 40, paragraph 7, that 'in the case of a county school the collective worship required in the school ... shall be wholly or mainly of a broadly Christian character ... (which) reflects the broad traditions of Christian belief without being distinctive of any particular Christian denomination'.[3]

However, despite this attempt at making what was implicit in the 1944 Act more explicit, these requirements were criticised by some for being unclear. What, for example, does 'broadly Christian' mean? Such a question is especially relevant to pupils and staff of non-Christian faiths, or those who don't belong to a religious tradition.

Nevertheless despite this perceived lack of clarity and some concern over the 'Christianising' of the 'assembly', it is arguable that the Act didn't, in practice, cause primary schools too many concerns. Ofsted has consistently reported that a majority of secondary schools are breaking the law with regard to collective worship but this is not the reported picture in primary schools.[4]

Despite this the Circular 1/94 has continued to be unpopular. The circular sought to make the requirements of the 1988 Act even more specific. It referred to the act of worship containing elements which 'accord a special status to Jesus Christ (paragraph 63) and being 'concerned with reverence or veneration paid to a divine being or power' (paragraph 57). What is interesting about this circular is that it appears to want to narrow the definition of collective worship in schools at a time when society at large is developing ever expanding views of spirituality and a plural and multi-faith approach to RE is firmly established in schools.

In the period since 1994 various organisations including the National Association of Head Teachers and The National Association of SACREs [5] have surveyed their members and found increasing evidence that this circular is unpopular. Such discontent resulted in a nation-wide consultation in 1997 called *Collective Worship Reviewed*. A report was published and is worth consulting.[6]

Collective worship: statutory requirements

The important sections of the 1988 Education Reform Act concerning collective worship state:

- There must be a daily act of collective worship for all pupils.

- In county schools it must be non-denominational and in other schools it may be in accordance with the foundation.

- Daily collective worship may be organised for separate groups of pupils at any time during the school day.

- These groups may be any group in which pupils are taught or take part in other school activities but not 'religious' groups.

- Responsibility for arranging collective worship at a county school lies with the headteacher; at a voluntary school, with the governing body.

- All acts of collective worship should take place on the school premises but the governing bodies of aided and special agreement schools have discretion to organise collective worship elsewhere.

- Acts of worship in a county school must be of a broadly Christian character, reflecting the broad traditions of Christian belief, and have regard for the age, aptitude and family background of pupils.

- Where it is difficult to reconcile the requirements for collective worship the Head may apply to SACRE for a determination that the requirement for broadly Christian collective worship should not apply to the school or a particular group of pupils within the school.

- SACRE can make a determination, which will last for 5 years. The Headteacher will be notified in writing. Where such a determination is made in respect of all or some of the pupils in the school, daily collective worship must still be provided for them, but may not be distinctive of a particular denomination. It may, however, be distinctive of a particular faith.

- Parents retain the right to withdraw their children from collective worship. This includes alternative worship as a result of a determination by SACRE.

- Teachers and Headteachers retain their right not to participate in acts of worship.

Figure 29: Statutory requirements for collective worship

Collective worship: towards an inclusive understanding

The report *Collective Worship Reviewed*, mentioned above, described three possible ways forward for collective worship. These are:

- Maintenance of the present requirements either entirely or substantially in their present form
- Withdrawal of the present requirements with no replacement
- A new approach which would support a statutory requirement for regular assemblies of a spiritual and moral character, with the present requirements for worship withdrawn. The intention behind this was to hold assemblies, which were inclusive, in which all could take part without the need for withdrawals.

It is interesting to note that the vast majority of organisations involved in the consultation favoured this new approach. However, at the time of writing, the government has seen fit not to make changes. It is unlikely, in the short term, that anything will be done to change the law on collective worship.

In the light of this then, it is an important, though difficult, task to be clear what your school understands by the term 'collective worship'. This section is intended to help you think through this issue.

What is the purpose of collective worship?

In a similar way to approaching the aims of RE (see Chapter 1) I often use the following exercise with teachers on in-service courses. Have a look at the statements in Figure 30 and see what you think about them.

Many schools are able to refer to LEA or Diocesan guidelines to help them with this. Check to see whether there is a document on collective worship available in your area.

It may be helpful to make some comments about the nature of collective worship, taking into account the above statements and the DfE Circular 1/94.

It is important to recognise the use of the term *collective* rather than *corporate*. This usage acknowledges the fact that pupils in school come from a variety of backgrounds. It cannot assume that any school grouping constitutes a 'body' of worshippers.

The word 'worship' is not defined in the 1988 Act or in any other legislation. Circular 1/94 has a section (paragraphs 57-59) where an attempt is made to discuss the meaning of collective worship. Those of you who have read this may have found it rather confusing. The circular recognises that worship in schools is by necessity of a different character than that which takes place amongst a group with beliefs in common.

Collective worship is a time for ...

• encouraging pupils to arrive at clearly held positions of faith

• allowing pupils to express and bear witness to their faith in a school setting

• increasing the sensitivity of pupils to the mystery of life and reflecting upon it

• maintaining whole school unity by admiring the work of classes and individuals, applauding sports results and hearing school notices

• complying with the 1988 Act by singing hymns and saying prayers

• helping pupils understand worship so that they may gain insight into what it is like to live a religious life

• putting over moral points

• giving staff or outside speakers who have a faith commitment the opportunity to share it with the pupils

---

Figure 30: Debating points for discussing collective worship in school

However, in paragraph 57 it states that worship should be taken to have its natural and ordinary meaning. This, as the circular recognises in paragraph 50, usually means worshipping God or at least something or someone who is thought to transcend ordinary existence. It is therefore assumed that while a group or school of pupils may not all belong to one religious tradition they do, however, all recognise the reality people call God as being worthy of worship.

This quite clearly is not the case. Many of our pupils do not come from backgrounds where God or divine reality is recognised. Therefore it cannot be appropriate, even if it were possible, to compel pupils to worship. However, the circular does recommend that worship elicit a response from pupils, that there should be more than passive attendance. At the same time, the circular recognises that some pupils may not be able to identify with an act of worship.

It is at this point that you may wish to throw up your arms in despair. It would be possible to get ourselves thoroughly confused and depressed. After all, it is schools that have to make this work.

One way forward is to look again at the statements above and see if we can clear a path through the forest of collective worship. Quite clearly it is not appropriate in a county school to encourage pupils to arrive at clearly held positions of faith if clearly held religious beliefs is what is meant. As we have seen earlier in the book, faith is a complex word, its definition ranging from strict adherence to a set of religious beliefs to a broadly human experience of seeking and finding meaning in life. Whatever the case, however, it is important that pupils are allowed to express their faith in a school setting if they are required to attend collective worship. Of course the parents of children with a particular faith may decide to withdraw them.

The third statement in the activity list above is concerned with increasing the sensitivity of pupils to the mystery in life and reflecting upon it. This sounds very grand but what does it mean? What we may be talking about here is what others have called the threshold of worship. This has something to do with recognising human beings' need to respond in some way to experience. It may be concerned with the big issues of life like suffering, or what it is to be happy, or who is my neighbour. It may be concerned with responding to the beauty of the natural world or the pain and beauty of relationships. What is particularly helpful about this view is that worship can be conceptualised as a response to experience, which can involve pupils in such activities as singing and praising, being thankful, giving to others, reflecting, being sorry etc. These activities in some ways relate to specifically religious activities that take place in places of worship but, instead of being focused on one particular view of experience that demands a particular set of beliefs, they can be expressions of all our pupils' responses to experience.

Yes – but, you may say, doesn't the law maintain that worship should be broadly Christian? It does, but what that means is difficult to define even though the circular refers to worship's according a special status to the person of Jesus Christ. What it doesn't mean, however, is that to comply with the 1988 Act a school must restrict its 'worship' to singing hymns and saying prayers. This would be to confuse the rituals of worship with worship itself. However, we cannot avoid the discussion of values when considering collective worship. Obviously a school will want to promote its agreed values, and the times when the school meets together is a good time for this. Often these values may be seen as broadly Christian; some may want to say that these are values, which are at the essence of other religious traditions as well. Values such as love and compassion, fairness and justice can all be promoted at this time.

However, this is not quite the same as putting across moral points, which sounds rather authoritarian with little opportunity for pupil reflection. Of course, there may be times when a firm line over some incident in school may be necessary.

Most schools will recognise the importance of the statement that begins with the words 'maintaining whole school unity'. This time in the school day has always been seen as a time for celebrating the positive aspects and values of school life. However, when drawing up a policy for collective worship it is important to take note of the circular when it makes a distinction between the assembly and collective worship (paragraph 58).

The final statement, concerning staff or outside speakers who have a faith commitment who may wish to share it with pupils, has positive and negative potential for collective worship. The positive side is that it is good for pupils to gain insight into what it means to live a religious life. This is all part of a meaningful religious education. However, this should not be seen as a free ticket for all and sundry to manipulate the situation and the pupils by evangelising or pushing a particular faith position.

Collective worship is a complex and sensitive area. As we mentioned at the beginning of the chapter, some have spoken out recently against the emphasis put on collective worship in the circular. What we have tried to do here is to help you confront some of the difficult issues so that an approach to collective worship can be taken that does not compromise the integrity of those involved while being educational at the same time.

By way of summary we can list several purposes for collective worship, which may help you in forming your approach.

Acts of collective worship can ...

- foster a sense of fellowship by bringing pupils together to celebrate shared values of the school and the community

- foster a sense of wonder and awe at the beauty, mystery and power of the world

- allow reflection on the fundamental questions of life and focus attention away from the concerns of the moment to those things which are of eternal concern to human beings

- provide an opportunity for celebration and thanksgiving and sharing of emotions such as love, joy, hope, friendship, acceptance, anguish, fear, reverence, forgiveness, etc

- foster a concern for the needs of other people

- provide a time for sharing successes and failures in personal, school and community life

- foster new insights about life and foster empathy for others

---

Figure 31: Educational opportunities provided by collective worship

Collective worship: practical issues

What follows in this section are some brief comments about practical issues regarding collective worship. As mentioned above, many local education authorities have produced very helpful documents about collective worship in their schools. These are usually particularly helpful over matters of practical importance. It is well worth enquiring about such a document if you do not already possess one.

Organisation

The 1988 Act allows you to organise collective worship in a variety of ways. This reflects not only a realism over organisational matters but also a genuine educational point: sometimes, preparing worship for a school that includes pupils ranging from 4 years to 11 years old can be taxing on the most creative mind. By allowing you to organise worship for a variety of school groupings, the Act allows you to prepare worship that can be meaningful for all involved.

To help you think about this we suggest a variety of organisational approaches.

- Whole school worship/assembly, led by head or senior member of staff, and may include outside speakers

- Whole school worship/assembly led by class teachers, perhaps on a rota

- Whole school worship/assembly led by class groups and involving the pupils in planning and leading the act

- Class based worship under the guidance and supervision of each class teacher

- In some schools, house assemblies

- Special assemblies: e.g. hymn practice, news assembly, worship in church on a special day, good work assembly, etc

---

Figure 32: Ways of organising collective worship

Content

How can you decide what is appropriate content for collective worship? A first step is to be clear about what the focus is of a particular act of worship. Check again the list on page 120.

Where might themes for worship come from?

- In some schools a majority of acts of worship may derive their themes from the range of faiths represented in the school. For example, a theme on spring may include Chinese New Year and Holi as explicit festivals, or a general theme such as the environment may draw on appropriate stories from the faiths represented in the school.
- A good source of themes for assembly can be derived from areas of shared human experience which pose fundamental or ultimate questions. Such questions were discussed in Chapters 2 and 3 and illustrations of human experience themes were given in Figure 12 (page 41). These examples can be very useful for planning meaningful and inclusive acts of collective worship.
- If your LEA has a published document on collective worship, it will very probably have some advice or examples on themes for worship. Contact your local RE Inspector or Education Office.

Elements

Acts of collective worship can include many elements, particularly in regard to rituals: for example, the use of music and hymns, the use of sacred scripture, using reflection techniques and prayer. There are a number of issues concerning these elements which are worth highlighting.

1 Music, songs, hymns
Music can contribute positively and in various ways to collective worship.

- It can set the scene and help create an appropriate atmosphere which is relevant to the theme
- It can be listened to, which can help pupils reflect and respond to a theme
- It can be played or sung, which can enable participants to express feelings that are not easily formulated in words.

Points to be aware of
- As school worship is an educational activity, make sure any hymns or songs chosen are appropriate to the age, aptitude and background of the pupil.
- Be aware of different religious traditions' stance on music. For example, many Muslims do not include music in worship.

2 Sacred Scripture

All sacred scriptures, in a real sense, belong to and have their context within a particular religious community. Often they can only, or at least best, be understood within that worshipping community. They also often express religious truths in a non-literal, symbolic or metaphorical way. It is important, therefore, to make sure you select appropriately from the scriptures. The following points are worth noting:

- Choose only stories/passages that are appropriate to the age and aptitude of your pupils.
- Make sure their use is in harmony with the overall theme and does not, as far as you understand it, distort the passage which has its proper place within its religious community.
- It is best to choose stories/passages that express truths or issues that are appropriate for people from a variety of religious backgrounds.

3 Reflection Techniques

We have already noted that music can play an important part in setting the atmosphere for an act of collective worship. There are also a number of other ways of creating an atmosphere and guiding reflection. These may include:

- closing the eyes to aid thinking and concentration
- lighting a candle to begin a story or to provide a focus of attention
- using flowers, plants or other natural objects, to help think about the beauty of the world
- using art or artefacts to help thought and reflection on human achievement
- bringing in animals to help with thoughts about caring for all creatures.

4 Prayer

To most people prayer is the central part of worship. Indeed to some, prayer and worship are the same thing. There are various kinds of prayers that can be used in acts of collective worship, including thanksgiving, intercession, petition, invocation and penitence. It should be remembered that prayer can involve words but doesn't necessarily have to. Prayer can often be a still and quiet reflection. Children can be invited to pray by focusing their attention on such stimuli as outlined in the previous section. Set, formal prayers can be used from the religious traditions but care is needed in selecting these. Are such selections appropriate and accessible to all taking part? Will some prayers exclude/offend some children?

It is also important to be aware of the rituals of prayer. It may well not be appropriate in many of today's schools to begin prayer time with the old saying 'Hands together and eyes closed'. Not only does this limit prayerful response (prayer is often easiest with the eyes open!) but it fails to respect the fact that people from various religious traditions have different positions that they assume for prayer. For example, Hindus may stand with hands together and eyes open, Muslims may prostrate themselves or kneel, and a Quaker may sit in silence.

Inspection and collective worship

It is generally agreed that collective worship has an important contribution to make to pupils' spiritual, moral, social and cultural development. Ofsted inspections will examine how far this is the case. Inspection requires that collective worship take place in all schools. For those county schools that are legally required to follow the local agreed syllabus for RE, inspectors must inspect the quality of collective worship. They should not visit acts of collective worship in voluntary schools, except where separately contracted to do so by the governing body. Governors of voluntary schools should arrange for denominational worship to be inspection. This is usually referred to as a Section 23 inspection.

[1] Hull, John, 'Can we speak of God or to God in education?', in *Dare We Speak of God in Public* (ed. F Young) Mowbray, 1995
[2] DfE: *Circular 1/94: Religious Education and Collective Worship*, 1994
[3] Education Reform Act, HMSO, 1988
[4] Ofsted, *Religious Education and Collective Worship* 1192-93
[5] For details of this see Geoff Teece, 'Collective worship: A new way forward' in *Primary Practice*, Number 15, May 1998
[6] Culham College Institute, *Collective Worship Reviewed*: Report of the 1997 Consultation, Culham 1998

Glossary: definitions of religious concepts

Buddhism

Anatta	no self; no soul. Denial of a real permanent self
Anicca	impermanence; transience. Instability of all things including the self
Buddha	awakened or enlightened one
Dhamma	universal law; ultimate truth. The teachings of the Buddha
Dukkha	suffering; unsatisfactoriness. The nature of existence according to the First Noble Truth
Kamma	action. Intentional actions that affect one's circumstances in this and future lives. The Buddha's insistence that the effect depends on volition marks the Buddhist understanding of kamma as different from the Hindu understanding of Karma
Metta	loving kindness. A pure love which is neither grasping nor possessive
Nibbana	blowing out of the fires of greed, hatred and ignorance, and the state of perfect peace that follows
Sangha	the community of fellowship of those who follow the teachings of Buddha
Tanha	thirst; craving; desire (rooted in ignorance). Desire as the cause of suffering. The Second Noble Truth

Christianity

Church	the whole community of Christians
Discipleship	following in the likeness of Christ
Faith	belief in certain truths; eg, the existence of God, God is love
God the Father	first person of the Holy Trinity. God is worshipped as creator, sustainer and judge of all

Holy Spirit	third person of the Holy Trinity. Active as divine presence and power in the world, and in dwelling in believers to make them like Christ and empower them to do God's will
Jesus Christ	the second person of the Holy Trinity. The central figure of Christian history and devotion
Love	highest Christian value, all other qualities flow from it. Greatest expression is in 1 Corinthians 13:4-7
Mission	God's activity in the world; also the call to Christians to proclaim the good news
Mother of God	the title given to the Virgin Mary, mainly in the Orthodox and Roman Catholic Churches, to underline the Trinitarian belief that Jesus was truly God
Resurrection	(i) the rising from the dead of Jesus Christ on the third day after the Crucifixion (ii) the rising from the dead of believers on the Last Day (iii) the new, or risen, life of Christians
Salvation	being saved from sin through the death and resurrection of Jesus
Sin	imperfect human condition, separation from God
Trinity	three persons in one God; Father, Son and Holy Spirit

Hinduism

Ahimsa	reverence for all living things
Atman	divine spark; ultimately the real self
Avatara	one who descends; sometimes translated as 'incarnation'; refers to the descent of a deity, most commonly Vishnu
Bhakti	devotion, love. Devotional form of Hinduism
Brahman	the ultimate reality, or the pervading reality; that from which everything emanates, in which it rests and into which it is ultimately dissolved
Dharma	religion or religious duty; that which sustains one's existence
Karma	action; law of cause and effect

Maya	illusion; when the permanent soul identifies itself with temporary matter eg the body
Moksha	ultimate liberation from the cycle of birth and death (*Samsara*)
Samsara	the world, the place where the soul passes through a series of lives, the wearisome wheel of life
Shakti	feminine divine power
Smriti	that which is heard, Hindu scriptures; specifically the four Vedas, including the Upanishads
Shruti	that which is remembered. Hindu scriptures, other than the Vedas
Varna	colour; the four principal divisions of Hindu society. It is important to note that the word caste refers strictly to sub-divisions within each Varna, and not to Varnas themselves
Yoga	communion; union of the soul with the Supreme, or a process which promotes that relationship. The English word yoke is derived from yoga

Islam

Akhirah	everlasting life after death, the hereafter
Allah	Islamic name for God in the Arabic language. Used in preference to the word God because the term is singular, has no plural and is not associated with masculine, feminine or neuter characteristics
Din	way of life, religion together with its practices
Ibadah	all acts of worship. Any permissible action performed with the intention to obey Allah
Iman	faith
Islam	peace attained through willing obedience to Allah's divine guidance
Jihad	personal individual struggle against evil in the way of Allah. It can also be the collective defence of the Muslim community

Qadar	Allah's complete and final control over the fulfilment of events or destiny
Qur'an	that which is read or recited. The Divine Book revealed to the Prophet Muhammad (*pbuh*). Allah's final revelation to human kind
Rasul	messenger of Allah
Salah	prescribed communication with, and worship of, Allah, performed under specific conditions, in the manner taught by the Prophet Muhammad (*pbuh*), and recited in the Arabic language. The five daily times of Salah are fixed by Allah
Shari'ah	Islamic law based upon the Qur'an and Sunnah
Shirk	association. Regarding anything as being equal or partner to Allah. It is forbidden in Islam
Sunnah	model practices, customs and traditions of the Prophet Muhammad (*pbuh*)
Tawhid	belief in the oneness of Allah; absolute monotheism
Ummah	community. Worldwide community of Muslims; the nation of Islam

Judaism

Brit	covenant; a relationship of mutual love and responsibility between God and humanity
Halakhah	literally, 'the way', the legal teachings of traditional Judaism
Israel	one who struggles with God. The phrase refers to the worldwide Jewish community; the land of Israel and the modern Jewish state of Israel
Kashrut	derived from Kasher; dietary laws
Mitzvah	individual unit of law prescribed in Torah
Shabbat	the Sabbath, celebrated from Friday sunset to Saturday evening
Shalom	peace
Synagogue	building for Jewish public prayer, study and assembly

Tanakh	Bible, an acronym made up of Torah, Nevi'im, and Ketuvim
Teshuvah	(literally) returning, repentance
Torah	the five books of Moses (narrow sense), the whole of traditional Jewish teaching (broad sense)
Tzedakah	(literally) justice, charity

Sikhism

Anand	bliss, the perfect state which defies description and can only be experienced
Grace	'the body takes birth because of Karma, but liberation is attained through God's grace' (AG2); the beginning of the liberation process through meditation on God's name, *nam simran*
Gurmukh	one who lives by the Guru's teachings
Guru	teacher; in Sikhism the title of Guru is reserved for the ten human Gurus and the Guru Granth Sahib
Haumai	egoism; the major spiritual defect
Ik Onkar	there is only One God. The first phrase of the Mool Mantra
Jivan Mukti	enlightened while in the material body; a spiritually enlightened person, freed from worldly bonds
Khalsa	the community of the pure; baptised Sikhs
Nam Simran	(literally) God remembrance; prayer or meditation, to hold God constantly in mind
Sewa	service; 'a place in God's Court can only be attained if we do service to others in this world' (AG26)
Sikh	learner, disciple; a person who believes in the ten Gurus and the Guru Granth Sahib

Bibliography

Useful general books for primary RE teachers

Bastide, Derek, *Co-ordinating Religious Education Across the Primary School*, Falmer Press, 1999

Bastide, Derek, *Religious Education 5–12*, Falmer Press, 1987

Blaylock, Lat and Johnson, Colin (eds), *A Teacher's Handbook of Religious Education*, CEM, 1997

Brown, Alan and Erica, *Religious Education in the Primary School*, National Society, 1996

Brown, Erica, *Religious Education for All*, David Fulton, 1996

Cole, Owen W and Evans-Lowndes, Judith, *Religious Education in the Primary Curriculum*, 2nd edition, RMEP, 1994

Copley, Terence, *Teaching Religion: Fifty Years of Religious Education in England and Wales*, University of Exeter Press, 1997

Copley, Terence and Gill, *Religious Education in Key Stage One: A Practical Guide*, Southgate, 1993

Copley, Terence (ed), *RE Futures*, PCfRE, 1998

Jackson, Robert, *Religious Education: an Interpretive Approach*, Hodder and Stoughton, 1997

Read, Garth et al, *How Do I teach RE?*, Westhill College, 2nd edition, 1998 version

Teece, Geoff, *How to Write Your School Policy for RE* (1994) and *How to Write Your Scheme of Work for RE* (1996), Westhill RE Centre

Teece, Geoff, *Pocket Guide to the Curriculum: Religious Education*, Scholastic, 2001